MASTERING GAME DEVELOPMENT WITH PYGAME

From Basics to Advanced Techniques

2ND EDITION

Table of Contents

Preface 1
Chapter 1: Introduction to Game Development 1
   What is Game Development? 1
   Overview of Popular Game Engines 2
      Unity 2
      Unreal Engine 2
      Godot 2
      CryEngine 3
      PyGame 3
   History and Evolution of PyGame 3
      Early Days 3
      Community Contributions 3
      Expanding Capabilities 3
      Educational Use 3
      PyGame and Beyond 4
      Future Prospects 4
   Setting Up Your Development Environment 4
      Step 1: Install Python 4
      Step 2: Install PyGame 4
      Step 3: Choose a Code Editor 4
      Step 4: Verify Installation 5
      Step 5: Set Up Version Control 5
      Step 6: Create a Project Directory 5
      Step 7: Configure Your Environment 5
      Step 8: Explore PyGame Documentation 6
   First Steps in PyGame 6
      Creating a Basic Game Window 6
      Explanation 7
      Handling Events 7
      Drawing Shapes and Text 8
      Explanation 8
Chapter 2: Python Programming Essentials 9
   Basics of Python Programming 9

- **Variables and Data Types** 9
- **Basic Operations** 10
- **Control Flow Statements** 10
- **Functions** 11
- **Modules** 11
- **Error Handling** 12
- **Conclusion** 12
- **Data Types and Structures** 12
  - **Primitive Data Types** 12
  - **Lists** 13
  - **Tuples** 13
  - **Sets** 14
  - **Dictionaries** 14
  - **String Manipulation** 15
  - **Conclusion** 15
- **Control Flow Statements** 15
  - **If Statements** 16
  - **For Loops** 16
  - **While Loops** 17
  - **Break and Continue** 17
  - **Nested Loops** 18
  - **List Comprehensions** 19
  - **Conclusion** 19
- **Functions and Modules** 19
  - **Defining Functions** 19
  - **Function Parameters and Return Values** 19
  - **Default Parameters** 20
  - **Variable-Length Arguments** 20
  - **Modules** 21
  - **Importing Specific Functions** 21
  - **Organizing Code with Packages** 22
  - **Conclusion** 22
- **Error Handling and Debugging** 22
  - **Exceptions and Error Handling** 23
  - **Custom Exceptions** 23
  - **Debugging** 24

Logging	24
Using Assertions	25
Conclusion	25
Chapter 3: Understanding PyGame Basics	25
Installing PyGame	25
PyGame Structure and Components	27
Creating a Basic Game Window	28
Handling Events in PyGame	30
Drawing Shapes and Text	33
Chapter 4: Game Graphics and Design	35
Introduction to Game Art and Design	35
Using Images and Sprites in PyGame	37
Animating Sprites	41
Managing Sprite Groups	45
Designing Your Game's Visuals	48
Art Style	48
Characters and Sprites	48
Backgrounds and Environments	48
User Interface	48
Visual Effects	49
Color Scheme	49
Animation	49
Consistency	49
Iteration	49
Tools	49
Example: Creating a Character Sprite	49
Integrating Visuals into PyGame	50
Chapter 5: Handling User Input	50
Keyboard Input	50
Mouse Input	54
Joystick and Gamepad Input	57
Creating Custom Controls	60
Step 1: Define Control Mappings	61
Step 2: Create a Control Handler	61
Step 3: Integrate Control Handler into Game Loop	61
Step 4: Adding Mouse Controls	63

Step 5: Adding Joystick Controls 63
Managing Input Events 64
Understanding the Event Queue 64
Centralized Event Handling 65
Advanced Event Management 66
Managing Multiple Input Sources 67
Chapter 6: Sound and Music in Games 69
Adding Sound Effects 69
Initializing the Mixer 69
Loading Sound Effects 70
Playing Sound Effects 70
Controlling Sound Playback 71
Using Multiple Sound Channels 72
Incorporating Background Music 73
Loading Background Music 73
Playing Background Music 74
Controlling Music Playback 75
Using Multiple Music Tracks 76
Managing Sound Channels 78
Understanding Sound Channels 78
Setting Up Sound Channels 78
Playing Sounds on Specific Channels 78
Controlling Sound Channels 80
Using Channel Reservations 81
Using Third-Party Sound Libraries 83
Overview of Popular Libraries 83
Integrating Pyglet with PyGame 83
Integrating PyAudio with PyGame 84
Integrating SoundFile with PyGame 85
Optimizing Audio for Performance 87
Reducing Audio Latency 87
Preloading Sounds 88
Using Audio Formats Efficiently 89
Managing Sound Channels Efficiently 89
Chapter 7: Game Physics and Collision Detection 91
Basic Physics Principles in Games 91

Implementing Gravity and Movement	92
Collision Detection Techniques	95
Handling Collisions and Responses	97
Advanced Physics Simulations	100
Chapter 8: Creating Game Levels	**103**
Designing Game Levels	103
Using Tile Maps	105
Implementing Level Transitions	108
Creating and Managing Level Data	111
Level Testing and Optimization	115
Level Testing and Optimization	118
Chapter 9: Character Development and AI	**122**
Designing Player Characters	122
Creating Non-Player Characters (NPCs)	123
Basic AI Concepts	124
Implementing Pathfinding	127
Advanced AI Behaviors	129
Chapter 10: Game State Management	**132**
Understanding Game States	132
Implementing Menus and HUDs	135
Saving and Loading Game Progress	137
Managing Game Loops	139
State Transition Management	143
Chapter 11: Multiplayer Game Development	**146**
Introduction to Multiplayer Games	146
Types of Multiplayer Games	146
Key Components of Multiplayer Games	146
Challenges in Multiplayer Game Development	146
Choosing a Networking Model	147
Tools and Frameworks	147
Example: Basic Networked Game	147
Network Programming Basics	148
Understanding Networking Protocols	148
Sockets and Connections	148
Creating a Basic Server	148
Creating a Basic Client	149

- Handling Multiple Clients 149
- Using Asynchronous Programming 150
- Example: Asynchronous Server 150
- Example: Asynchronous Client 151
- Conclusion 151

Setting Up a Server-Client Architecture 151
- Server-Client Model Overview 151
- Designing the Server 152
- Implementing the Server 152
- Designing the Client 153
- Implementing the Client 153
- Handling Game State Synchronization 154
- Implementing State Synchronization 154
- Conclusion 155

Handling Real-Time Multiplayer 155
- Real-Time Multiplayer Challenges 155
- Techniques for Reducing Latency 155
- Implementing Client-Side Prediction 155
- Dead Reckoning Technique 156
- Lag Compensation 157
- Synchronizing Game State 157
- Example: Delta Updates 157
- Implementing Real-Time Multiplayer with WebSockets 158
- Example: WebSocket Server with `websockets` 158
- Example: WebSocket Client 159
- Conclusion 159

Synchronizing Game States 159
- Importance of Game State Synchronization 159
- Techniques for Synchronizing Game States 160
- State Replication 160
- Example: State Replication 160
- Delta Updates 161
- Example: Delta Updates 161
- Event-Based Updates 162
- Example: Event-Based Updates 162

- Handling Network Latency 162
- Example: Client-Side Prediction 163
- Conclusion 163

Chapter 12: Enhancing Game Performance 164

Profiling and Optimization Techniques 164
- Importance of Profiling 164
- Profiling Tools 164
- Using cProfile 164
- Line-by-Line Profiling with line_profiler 165
- Identifying Bottlenecks 165
- Optimizing Code 166
- Example: Code Refactoring 166
- Efficient Data Structures 166
- Caching Techniques 167
- Asynchronous Programming 167
- Conclusion 168

Memory Management 168
- Understanding Memory Usage 168
- Identifying Memory Leaks 168
- Tools for Monitoring Memory Usage 168
- Using the gc Module 168
- Using objgraph 169
- Using memory_profiler 169
- Managing Memory Allocation 170
- Example: Object Pooling 170
- Example: Lazy Initialization 170
- Conclusion 171

Reducing Lag and Latency 171
- Understanding Lag and Latency 171
- Causes of Lag and Latency 171
- Techniques for Reducing Lag 172
- Optimizing Network Code 172
- Example: Data Compression 172
- Example: Predictive Algorithms 172
- Load Balancing 173
- Example: Horizontal Scaling 173

- Client-Side Optimization ... 174
- Example: Efficient Rendering ... 174
- Conclusion ... 174
- **Efficient Rendering Strategies** ... 175
  - Understanding Rendering ... 175
  - Techniques for Efficient Rendering ... 175
  - Batch Rendering ... 175
  - Example: Batch Rendering in Pygame ... 175
  - Level of Detail (LOD) ... 176
  - Example: Level of Detail ... 176
  - Frustum Culling ... 177
  - Example: Frustum Culling ... 177
  - Occlusion Culling ... 178
  - Example: Occlusion Culling ... 178
  - Conclusion ... 179
- **Optimizing for Different Platforms** ... 179
  - Understanding Platform Differences ... 179
  - Common Platforms ... 179
  - Techniques for Platform Optimization ... 179
  - Conditional Compilation ... 180
  - Resource Management ... 180
  - Example: Lazy Loading ... 180
  - Input Handling ... 181
  - Example: Touch Controls ... 181
  - Performance Profiling ... 182
  - Example: Platform-Specific Profiling Tools ... 182
  - Conclusion ... 182
- Conclusion ... 182

Chapter 13: Implementing Game UI ... 183
- Designing User Interfaces ... 183
- Creating Menus and Buttons ... 184
- Integrating UI with Game Logic ... 186
- Responsive UI Design ... 187
- User Experience Testing ... 188

Chapter 14: Advanced Graphics Techniques ... 188
- Working with 2D Graphics ... 189

Introduction to 3D Graphics in PyGame ... 191
Shaders and Special Effects ... 192
Lighting and Shadows ... 194
Procedural Content Generation ... 196

Chapter 15: Building a Game Engine ... 197
Understanding Game Engines ... 197
Core Components of a Game Engine ... 198
- Rendering Engine ... 198
- Physics Engine ... 199
- Audio Engine ... 199
- Input System ... 199
- Scripting Engine ... 199
- Animation System ... 199
- Artificial Intelligence (AI) ... 199
- Networking ... 199
- Memory Management ... 199
- Debugging and Profiling Tools ... 199

Designing Your Engine Architecture ... 200
- Modular Design ... 200
- Component-Based Architecture ... 200
- Entity-Component-System (ECS) ... 200
- Event-Driven Architecture ... 200
- Data-Driven Design ... 200

Implementing Engine Features ... 200
- Rendering ... 200
- Physics ... 200
- Audio ... 201
- Input ... 201
- Scripting ... 201
- Animation ... 201
- AI ... 201
- Networking ... 201
- Memory Management ... 201
- Debugging and Profiling ... 201

Testing and Debugging Your Engine ... 201
- Unit Testing ... 202

- Integration Testing 202
- Performance Testing 202
- User Testing 202
- Continuous Integration 202
- Core Components of a Game Engine 202
  - Rendering Engine 202
  - Physics Engine 202
  - Audio Engine 203
  - Input System 203
  - Scripting Engine 203
  - Animation System 203
  - Networking 203
  - Memory Management 203
  - Debugging Tools 203
- Designing Your Engine Architecture 204
  - Modular Design 204
  - Component-Based Architecture 204
  - Event-Driven Architecture 204
  - Data-Driven Design 204
  - Entity-Component-System (ECS) Pattern 204
- Implementing Engine Features 204
  - Rendering Engine 204
  - Physics Engine 205
  - Audio Engine 205
  - Input System 205
  - Scripting Engine 205
  - Animation System 205
  - AI 205
  - Networking 205
  - Memory Management 206
  - Debugging and Profiling 206
- Testing and Debugging Your Engine 206
  - Unit Testing 206
  - Integration Testing 206
  - Performance Testing 206
  - User Testing 206

- Continuous Integration 206
- Implementing Engine Features 207
  - Rendering Engine 207
  - Physics Engine 208
  - Audio Engine 208
  - Input System 208
  - Scripting Engine 208
  - Animation System 209
  - AI 209
  - Networking 209
  - Memory Management 210
  - Debugging and Profiling 210
- Testing and Debugging Your Engine 210
  - Unit Testing 210
  - Integration Testing 210
  - Performance Testing 211
  - User Testing 211
  - Continuous Integration 211
- Chapter 16: Integrating Third-Party Libraries 211
  - Overview of Useful Libraries 211
    - Pyglet 211
    - OpenGL 211
    - Box2D 212
    - FMOD 212
    - TensorFlow 212
    - SDL 212
    - ImGui 212
  - Integrating with Pyglet and OpenGL 212
    - Setting Up Pyglet 212
    - Integrating OpenGL 213
    - Handling Input with Pyglet 214
    - Loading Textures 214
    - Implementing Advanced Features 215
  - Using Physics Libraries 216
    - Setting Up Box2D 216
    - Creating a Physics World 216

- Simulating Physics 217
- Handling Collisions 217
- Incorporating AI Libraries 218
  - TensorFlow 218
  - Behavior Trees 219
  - Pathfinding 219
- Combining Multiple Libraries 220
  - Ensure Compatibility 220
  - Modular Design 220
  - Performance Optimization 220
  - Consistent Interfaces 220
  - Testing and Debugging 220

Chapter 17: Game Monetization Strategies 220

- Understanding Game Monetization 220
- In-Game Purchases and Ads 221
- Premium vs. Freemium Models 222
  - Premium Model 222
  - Freemium Model 223
  - Choosing the Right Model 223
- Marketing Your Game 224
  - 1. Identify Your Target Audience 224
  - 2. Create a Strong Brand 224
  - 3. Build a Website and Social Media Presence 224
  - 4. Leverage Influencers and Streamers 224
  - 5. Participate in Gaming Communities 224
  - 6. Run Paid Advertising Campaigns 225
  - 7. Create a Compelling Launch Campaign 225
  - 8. Analyze and Optimize 225
- Legal and Ethical Considerations 225
  - Legal Considerations 225
  - Ethical Considerations 225

Chapter 18: Game Testing and Quality Assurance 226

- Importance of Testing in Game Development 226
  - 1. Identifying Bugs and Glitches 226
  - 2. Ensuring Gameplay Balance 226
  - 3. Improving User Experience 226

- 4. Compatibility Testing 227
- 5. Performance Optimization 227
- 6. Compliance and Certification 227
- 7. Feedback and Iteration 227
- 8. Building Player Trust 227

Automated Testing Techniques 227
- 1. Unit Testing 227
- 2. Integration Testing 228
- 3. Regression Testing 228
- 4. Performance Testing 228
- 5. UI Testing 228
- 6. Load Testing 229
- 7. Continuous Integration 229

Bug Tracking and Management 229
- 1. Choosing a Bug Tracking Tool 229
- 2. Reporting Bugs 229
- 3. Prioritizing Bugs 229
- 4. Assigning Bugs 230
- 5. Tracking Bug Status 230
- 6. Testing Bug Fixes 230
- 7. Communicating with the Team 230
- 8. Analyzing Bug Trends 230
- 9. Continuous Improvement 230

User Testing and Feedback 230
- 1. Defining Testing Objectives 231
- 2. Selecting Testers 231
- 3. Creating Test Scenarios 231
- 4. Conducting Playtests 231
- 5. Gathering Feedback 231
- 6. Analyzing Feedback 231
- 7. Iterating on Feedback 231
- 8. Involving the Community 232
- 9. Balancing Player Expectations 232
- 10. Continuous Improvement 232

Ensuring Game Quality 232
- 1. Establish Quality Standards 232

    2. Create a Testing Plan 232

    3. Automate Testing 232

    4. Conduct Regular Playtests 233

    5. Monitor Performance Metrics 233

    6. Address Bugs Promptly 233

    7. Optimize User Experience 233

    8. Ensure Cross-Platform Compatibility 233

    9. Verify Compliance 233

    10. Document Processes 233

    11. Foster a Quality Culture 234

  Post-Release Support and Updates 234

    1. Monitor Player Feedback 234

    2. Release Regular Updates 234

    3. Address Critical Issues 234

    4. Introduce New Content 234

    5. Balance Gameplay 234

    6. Communicate with Players 234

    7. Implement Quality Assurance 235

    8. Analyze Player Data 235

    9. Offer Limited-Time Events 235

    10. Plan for Longevity 235

Chapter 19: Publishing and Distribution 235

  Preparing Your Game for Release 235

  Choosing Distribution Platforms 236

  Managing Digital Rights and DRM 237

  Marketing and Promotion 238

  Post-Release Support and Updates 239

Chapter 20: Case Studies and Future Trends 240

  Successful PyGame Projects 240

  Lessons Learned from Indie Developers 241

  Emerging Trends in Game Development 242

  The Future of PyGame 243

  Continuing Your Game Development Journey 245

Preface

Welcome to the fascinating world of game development with Python and PyGame! This book is designed to take you on a journey from the basics of Python programming to the advanced techniques required to build your own game engine. Whether you are a beginner or an experienced developer, you will find valuable insights and practical advice to help you create engaging and high-performance games.

Game development is a multidisciplinary field that combines creativity, technical skills, and a deep understanding of game mechanics. This book covers a wide range of topics, from the fundamentals of Python programming to the intricacies of game physics, AI, and multiplayer development. Each chapter is designed to build on the previous one, gradually introducing more complex concepts and techniques.

We begin with an introduction to game development and an overview of popular game engines. You will learn about the history and evolution of PyGame, set up your development environment, and take your first steps in PyGame. From there, we delve into the essentials of Python programming, covering data types, control flow, functions, modules, and error handling.

As you progress through the chapters, you will gain a deep understanding of PyGame's structure and components, learn how to handle user input, manage game states, and optimize game performance. You will explore advanced topics such as game physics, AI, multiplayer development, and the integration of third-party libraries. The book also covers game monetization strategies, testing, quality assurance, and publishing your game.

Throughout the book, you will find practical examples and code snippets to help you understand and apply the concepts. By the end of this journey, you will have the knowledge and skills to create your own games and even build your own game engine.

Thank you for choosing this book as your guide to game development with Python and PyGame. Let's embark on this exciting adventure together and turn your game development dreams into reality!

Chapter 1: Introduction to Game Development

What is Game Development?

Game development is the process of creating interactive entertainment experiences, commonly known as video games. It encompasses a wide range of disciplines, including programming, art, design, sound, and testing. At its core, game development involves designing gameplay mechanics, creating assets, writing code, and integrating everything into a cohesive, engaging experience for players.

The development process typically starts with an idea or concept, which is then expanded into a detailed game design document. This document outlines the game's mechanics, story, characters, levels, and other elements. From there, developers begin creating the game by developing prototypes, iterating on gameplay, and refining the overall experience.

Game development can be done by individuals or large teams, depending on the scope and complexity of the project. Indie developers often work solo or in small teams, while AAA games are created by large studios with hundreds of team members. Regardless of the size of the team, successful game development requires collaboration, creativity, and a solid understanding of the various components that make up a game.

Python, with its simplicity and readability, has become a popular language for game development, especially for beginners and indie developers. PyGame, a library built on top of Python, provides a powerful framework for creating 2D games. It simplifies many aspects of game development, such as handling graphics, sound, and user input, allowing developers to focus on designing and coding their games.

Overview of Popular Game Engines

A game engine is a software framework designed to facilitate game development. It provides essential tools and libraries for rendering graphics, processing input, managing assets, and implementing game logic. Using a game engine can significantly speed up the development process and help developers create more polished and optimized games.

There are several popular game engines available, each with its own strengths and weaknesses. Some of the most widely used game engines include:

Unity

Unity is one of the most popular game engines, known for its versatility and ease of use. It supports both 2D and 3D game development and provides a wide range of features, including physics simulation, animation, networking, and a robust asset pipeline. Unity uses

C# as its primary scripting language, making it accessible to developers with a background in C-like languages.

Unreal Engine

Unreal Engine is a powerful game engine developed by Epic Games. It is widely used in the industry for creating high-quality 3D games. Unreal Engine offers advanced rendering capabilities, a comprehensive physics engine, and a visual scripting system called Blueprints. It uses C++ for scripting, providing developers with fine-grained control over their games.

Godot

Godot is an open-source game engine that supports both 2D and 3D game development. It is known for its user-friendly interface and flexible scene system. Godot uses its own scripting language called GDScript, which is similar to Python, making it easy to learn for Python developers. It also supports C# and C++ for more advanced scripting needs.

CryEngine

CryEngine is a high-performance game engine developed by Crytek. It is renowned for its cutting-edge graphics and realistic environments. CryEngine provides a comprehensive suite of tools for level design, animation, and audio. It uses C++ for scripting and offers a visual scripting system for non-programmers.

PyGame

PyGame is a Python library specifically designed for 2D game development. It provides modules for handling graphics, sound, input, and other game-related tasks. PyGame is ideal for beginners and hobbyists due to its simplicity and ease of use. While it may not have all the features of more advanced engines, it is a great starting point for learning game development and creating smaller games.

Each of these game engines has its own strengths and is suited to different types of projects. The choice of engine depends on factors such as the complexity of the game, the target platform, the team's expertise, and the specific requirements of the project.

History and Evolution of PyGame

PyGame is a cross-platform library designed for making video games in Python. It was created by Pete Shinners in 2000 as a wrapper around the Simple DirectMedia Layer (SDL) library, which provides low-level access to audio, keyboard, mouse, and graphics hardware.

Early Days

The initial release of PyGame provided basic functionality for game development, allowing developers to create simple 2D games with minimal setup. Over time, PyGame grew in popularity within the Python community, thanks to its ease of use and the increasing interest in Python as a programming language.

Community Contributions

One of the key strengths of PyGame is its open-source nature. The community has played a significant role in its development, contributing bug fixes, new features, and improvements. This collaborative effort has helped PyGame remain relevant and up-to-date with the latest advancements in game development.

Expanding Capabilities

As PyGame evolved, new modules and functionalities were added. These include advanced sound support, sprite handling, collision detection, and support for various image formats. The library also improved its performance and compatibility with different platforms, making it a robust choice for 2D game development.

Educational Use

PyGame has become a popular tool for teaching programming and game development. Its simplicity and clear syntax make it an excellent choice for beginners. Many educational institutions and online courses use PyGame to introduce students to the basics of programming and game design.

PyGame and Beyond

While PyGame remains focused on 2D game development, it has inspired the creation of other Python-based game development libraries and frameworks. Libraries such as Arcade and Pyglet offer alternative approaches and additional features, catering to different needs within the game development community.

Future Prospects

The future of PyGame looks promising, with ongoing development and community support. As Python continues to grow in popularity, PyGame is likely to attract new developers and maintain its position as a go-to library for 2D game development in Python.

Setting Up Your Development Environment

Setting up your development environment is a crucial step in starting your journey with PyGame. This involves installing the necessary software, configuring your tools, and ensuring everything is working correctly. Here's a step-by-step guide to get you started:

Step 1: Install Python

First, you need to have Python installed on your system. PyGame is compatible with Python 3, so it's recommended to install the latest version of Python 3 from the official Python website (https://www.python.org/). Follow the installation instructions for your operating system.

Step 2: Install PyGame

Once Python is installed, you can install PyGame using the Python package manager, pip. Open your terminal or command prompt and run the following command:

```
pip install pygame
```

This will download and install the latest version of PyGame and its dependencies.

Step 3: Choose a Code Editor

Next, you need a code editor or an integrated development environment (IDE) to write your game code. Some popular options include:

- **Visual Studio Code**: A powerful, open-source code editor with extensive language support and extensions.
- **PyCharm**: A feature-rich IDE specifically designed for Python development.
- **Sublime Text**: A lightweight, fast code editor with support for multiple programming languages.

Choose the one that best fits your needs and preferences.

Step 4: Verify Installation

To verify that PyGame is installed correctly, create a new Python file (e.g., `test_pygame.py`) and add the following code:

```
import pygame
pygame.init()
print("PyGame initialized successfully!")
```

Run the script using your code editor or terminal. If you see the message "PyGame initialized successfully!", your setup is complete.

Step 5: Set Up Version Control

Using version control is a good practice in software development. Git is a popular version control system that allows you to track changes, collaborate with others, and manage your codebase efficiently. Install Git from the official website (https://git-scm.com/) and set up a repository for your project.

Step 6: Create a Project Directory

Create a directory for your PyGame project. This will be the root directory where you organize your code, assets, and other resources. For example:

```
my_game/
├── assets/
│   ├── images/
│   ├── sounds/
├── src/
│   ├── main.py
├── README.md
├── .gitignore
```

Step 7: Configure Your Environment

Configure your code editor or IDE to recognize your project directory and set up any necessary extensions or plugins for Python and PyGame development. This might include syntax highlighting, code linting, and debugging tools.

Step 8: Explore PyGame Documentation

Familiarize yourself with the PyGame documentation (https://www.pygame.org/docs/). It provides comprehensive information about the library's modules, classes, and functions, along with examples and tutorials.

By following these steps, you'll have a well-prepared development environment for creating games with PyGame. This setup will help you focus on coding and developing your game without worrying about configuration issues.

First Steps in PyGame

With your development environment set up, it's time to take your first steps in PyGame. In this section, we'll create a simple game window and explore some basic functionalities of PyGame.

Creating a Basic Game Window

A game window is the primary interface where all the game action takes place. Let's start by creating a basic game window using PyGame.

Create a new Python file (e.g., `main.py`) in your project directory and add the following code:

```python
import pygame
import sys

# Initialize PyGame
pygame.init()

# Set up the game window
screen = pygame.display.set_mode((800, 600))
pygame.display.set_caption("My First PyGame Window")

# Main game loop
running = True
while running:
    for event in pygame.event.get():
        if event.type == pygame.QUIT:
            running = False

    # Fill the screen with a color (e.g., white)
    screen.fill((255, 255, 255))

    # Update the display
    pygame.display.flip()

# Quit PyGame
pygame.quit()
sys.exit()
```

Explanation

1. **Initializing PyGame**: We start by importing the necessary modules (pygame and sys) and initializing PyGame with pygame.init().
2. **Setting Up the Game Window**: We create a game window with a resolution of 800x600 pixels using pygame.display.set_mode(). The window's title is set using pygame.display.set_caption().
3. **Main Game Loop**: The main game loop keeps the game running. Inside the loop, we handle events, such as closing the window, by checking for pygame.QUIT. We fill the screen with a white color using screen.fill(), and update the display with pygame.display.flip().
4. **Quitting PyGame**: When the game loop ends, we quit PyGame with pygame.quit() and exit the program using sys.exit().

Run the script, and you should see a window titled "My First PyGame Window" with a white background. Congratulations! You've created your first PyGame window.

Handling Events

Handling events is a crucial part of game development. Events can include user inputs (keyboard, mouse, joystick), window actions (minimize, close), and custom game events. PyGame provides an event system to handle these events efficiently.

In the previous code, we handled the `pygame.QUIT` event to close the game window. Let's add more event handling to respond to keyboard inputs:

```
while running:
    for event in pygame.event.get():
        if event.type == pygame.QUIT:
            running = False
        elif event.type == pygame.KEYDOWN:
            if event.key == pygame.K_ESCAPE:
                running = False

    screen.fill((255, 255, 255))
    pygame.display.flip()
```

In this code, we handle the `pygame.KEYDOWN` event to check if the Escape key is pressed (`pygame.K_ESCAPE`). If it is, we set `running` to `False`, which exits the game loop and closes the window.

Drawing Shapes and Text

PyGame provides functions to draw shapes and render text on the screen. Let's draw a rectangle and display some text in our game window.

First, add the following code to the `main.py` file:

```
# Set up font
font = pygame.font.SysFont(None, 48)

while running:
    for event in pygame.event.get():
        if event.type == pygame.QUIT:
            running = False
        elif event.type == pygame.KEYDOWN:
            if event.key == pygame.K_ESCAPE:
                running = False
```

```
    screen.fill((255, 255, 255))

    # Draw a red rectangle
    pygame.draw.rect(screen, (255, 0, 0), (100, 100, 200, 100))

    # Render and display text
    text = font.render("Hello, PyGame!", True, (0, 0, 0))
    screen.blit(text, (100, 250))

    pygame.display.flip()
```

Explanation

1. **Setting Up Font**: We create a font object using `pygame.font.SysFont()`, specifying the font name and size.
2. **Drawing a Rectangle**: We use `pygame.draw.rect()` to draw a red rectangle on the screen. The rectangle's position and size are defined by a tuple `(x, y, width, height)`.
3. **Rendering and Displaying Text**: We render the text "Hello, PyGame!" using `font.render()`, specifying the text, anti-aliasing, and color. The rendered text is then displayed on the screen using `screen.blit()`.

Run the script, and you should see a red rectangle and the text "Hello, PyGame!" displayed in the game window. This demonstrates the basics of drawing shapes and rendering text in PyGame.

These are your first steps in PyGame. As you continue, you'll explore more advanced features and techniques to create interactive and engaging games.

Chapter 2: Python Programming Essentials

Basics of Python Programming

Python is a versatile and beginner-friendly programming language known for its simplicity and readability. It has become a popular choice for various applications, including web development, data analysis, artificial intelligence, and game development. In this section, we will cover the basics of Python programming to ensure you have a solid foundation for using PyGame.

Variables and Data Types

In Python, variables are used to store data values. A variable is created by assigning a value to a name using the equals sign (=). Python supports various data types, including integers, floating-point numbers, strings, lists, and dictionaries.

```python
# Integer
age = 25

# Floating-point number
height = 5.9

# String
name = "Alice"

# List
colors = ["red", "green", "blue"]

# Dictionary
person = {"name": "Alice", "age": 25}
```

Basic Operations

Python supports basic arithmetic operations, such as addition, subtraction, multiplication, and division. You can also perform operations on strings and lists.

```python
# Arithmetic operations
a = 10
b = 5
print(a + b)   # Output: 15
```

```python
print(a - b)   # Output: 5
print(a * b)   # Output: 50
print(a / b)   # Output: 2.0

# String operations
greeting = "Hello"
name = "Alice"
message = greeting + " " + name
print(message)  # Output: Hello Alice

# List operations
numbers = [1, 2, 3]
numbers.append(4)
print(numbers)  # Output: [1, 2, 3, 4]
```

Control Flow Statements

Control flow statements are used to control the execution of code based on certain conditions. The most common control flow statements in Python are `if`, `for`, and `while` statements.

```python
# If statement
x = 10
if x > 5:
    print("x is greater than 5")
else:
    print("x is not greater than 5")

# For loop
for i in range(5):
    print(i)  # Output: 0, 1, 2, 3, 4

# While loop
count = 0
while count < 5:
    print(count)  # Output: 0, 1, 2, 3, 4
    count += 1
```

Functions

Functions are blocks of reusable code that perform a specific task. They are defined using the `def` keyword, followed by the function name and parameters.

```
def greet(name):
    return "Hello, " + name

print(greet("Alice"))   # Output: Hello, Alice
```

Modules

Modules are files containing Python code that can be imported and used in other Python programs. The standard library includes many useful modules, and you can also create your own.

```
# Importing a standard library module
import math
print(math.sqrt(16))   # Output: 4.0

# Creating and importing a custom module
# my_module.py
def add(a, b):
    return a + b

# main.py
import my_module
print(my_module.add(2, 3))   # Output: 5
```

Error Handling

Python provides mechanisms to handle errors and exceptions gracefully. The `try` and `except` blocks are used to catch and handle exceptions.

```
try:
    result = 10 / 0
except ZeroDivisionError:
    print("Cannot divide by zero")
```

Conclusion

Understanding these basics of Python programming is essential for working with PyGame. As you progress through this book, you will build on these fundamentals to create more complex and interactive games. Python's simplicity and readability make it an excellent choice for game development, allowing you to focus on designing and coding your games.

Data Types and Structures

Data types and structures are fundamental concepts in programming. They determine how data is stored, organized, and manipulated in a program. In Python, there are several built-in data types and structures that you will frequently use when developing games with PyGame.

Primitive Data Types

Python supports several primitive data types, including integers, floating-point numbers, strings, and booleans.

```
# Integer
score = 100

# Floating-point number
time_elapsed = 3.5

# String
player_name = "Alice"

# Boolean
is_game_over = False
```

Lists

Lists are ordered collections of items that can store elements of different data types. Lists are mutable, meaning their elements can be changed after they are created.

```
# Creating a list
inventory = ["sword", "shield", "potion"]

# Accessing list elements
print(inventory[0])   # Output: sword

# Modifying list elements
inventory[1] = "magic shield"
print(inventory)   # Output: ["sword", "magic shield", "potion"]

# Adding elements to a list
```

```
inventory.append("helmet")
print(inventory)   # Output: ["sword", "magic shield", "potion",
"helmet"]

# Removing elements from a list
inventory.remove("potion")
print(inventory)  # Output: ["sword", "magic shield", "helmet"]
```

Tuples

Tuples are ordered collections of items similar to lists, but they are immutable, meaning their elements cannot be changed after they are created.

```
# Creating a tuple
position = (10, 20)

# Accessing tuple elements
print(position[0])  # Output: 10

# Tuples are immutable
# position[0] = 15  # This will raise a TypeError
```

Sets

Sets are unordered collections of unique items. They are useful for storing elements where duplicates are not allowed.

```
# Creating a set
unique_items = {"sword", "shield", "potion"}

# Adding elements to a set
unique_items.add("helmet")
print(unique_items)    # Output: {"sword", "shield", "potion",
"helmet"}

# Removing elements from a set
unique_items.remove("potion")
print(unique_items)  # Output: {"sword", "shield", "helmet"}
```

Dictionaries

Dictionaries are collections of key-value pairs. They are unordered and mutable, allowing you to store and retrieve data using keys.

```python
# Creating a dictionary
player_stats = {"name": "Alice", "score": 100, "level": 5}

# Accessing dictionary elements
print(player_stats["name"])  # Output: Alice

# Modifying dictionary elements
player_stats["score"] = 150
print(player_stats)   # Output: {"name": "Alice", "score": 150, "level": 5}

# Adding elements to a dictionary
player_stats["health"] = 75
print(player_stats)   # Output: {"name": "Alice", "score": 150, "level": 5, "health": 75}

# Removing elements from a dictionary
del player_stats["level"]
print(player_stats)   # Output: {"name": "Alice", "score": 150, "health": 75}
```

String Manipulation

Strings are sequences of characters used to store and manipulate text. Python provides several methods for string manipulation.

```python
# Concatenation
greeting = "Hello, " + "World!"
print(greeting)  # Output: Hello, World!

# String formatting
name = "Alice"
formatted_string = f"Hello, {name}!"
print(formatted_string)  # Output: Hello, Alice!

# String methods
message = "   Hello, PyGame!   "
print(message.strip())  # Output: Hello, PyGame!
print(message.upper())  # Output: HELLO, PYGAME!
```

```
print(message.lower())    # Output: hello, pygame!
```

Conclusion

Understanding data types and structures is crucial for managing and manipulating data in your games. Whether you're storing player stats, managing inventory, or handling game states, these concepts will be fundamental to your game development process. As you become more familiar with these data types and structures, you'll be able to use them effectively to create more complex and interactive games.

Control Flow Statements

Control flow statements are fundamental constructs in programming that allow you to dictate the order in which code is executed. They enable you to make decisions, iterate over sequences, and control the flow of your program based on certain conditions. In this section, we will explore the essential control flow statements in Python.

If Statements

The `if` statement is used to execute a block of code only if a specified condition is true. If the condition is false, the code block is skipped.

```
score = 85

if score >= 90:
    print("Grade: A")
elif score >= 80:
    print("Grade: B")
elif score >= 70:
    print("Grade: C")
elif score >= 60:
    print("Grade: D")
else:
    print("Grade: F")
```

In this example, the code checks the value of `score` and prints the corresponding grade based on the condition.

For Loops

The `for` loop is used to iterate over a sequence (such as a list, tuple, string, or range) and execute a block of code for each element in the sequence.

```python
# Iterating over a list
inventory = ["sword", "shield", "potion"]
for item in inventory:
    print(item)

# Output:
# sword
# shield
# potion

# Using range()
for i in range(5):
    print(i)

# Output:
# 0
# 1
# 2
# 3
# 4
```

While Loops

The `while` loop is used to repeatedly execute a block of code as long as a specified condition is true.

```
count = 0
while count < 5:
    print(count)
    count += 1

# Output:
# 0
# 1
# 2
# 3
# 4
```

Break and Continue

The `break` statement is used to exit a loop prematurely, while the `continue` statement is used to skip the current iteration and proceed to the next iteration.

Copy code
```
# Using break
for i in range(10):
    if i == 5:
        break
    print(i)

# Output:
# 0
# 1
# 2
# 3
# 4

# Using continue
for i in range(10):
    if i % 2 == 0:
        continue
    print(i)

# Output:
# 1
# 3
# 5
# 7
# 9
```

Nested Loops

Loops can be nested within each other to perform more complex iterations. Nested loops are commonly used for tasks such as iterating over multi-dimensional arrays.

```
# Nested loop example
for i in range(3):
    for j in range(3):
        print(f"i: {i}, j: {j}")
```

```
# Output:
# i: 0, j: 0
# i: 0, j: 1
# i: 0, j: 2
# i: 1, j: 0
# i: 1, j: 1
# i: 1, j: 2
# i: 2, j: 0
# i: 2, j: 1
# i: 2, j: 2
```

List Comprehensions

List comprehensions provide a concise way to create lists using a single line of code. They are often used as an alternative to traditional loops.

```
# List comprehension
numbers = [1, 2, 3, 4, 5]
squares = [x ** 2 for x in numbers]
print(squares)  # Output: [1, 4, 9, 16, 25]
```

Conclusion

Control flow statements are essential for creating dynamic and responsive programs. They allow you to make decisions, iterate over data, and control the execution of your code. Understanding and effectively using control flow statements will enable you to build more complex and interactive games with PyGame.

Functions and Modules

Functions and modules are essential building blocks in Python that promote code reusability, organization, and modularity. Functions allow you to encapsulate code into reusable blocks, while modules enable you to organize your code into separate files and import them as needed. In this section, we will explore how to define and use functions and modules in Python.

Defining Functions

A function is defined using the `def` keyword, followed by the function name, parameters, and a colon. The function body contains the code to be executed when the function is called.

```python
def greet(name):
    print(f"Hello, {name}!")

# Calling the function
greet("Alice")  # Output: Hello, Alice!
```

Function Parameters and Return Values

Functions can accept parameters and return values. Parameters allow you to pass data to the function, and the `return` statement is used to return a value from the function.

```python
def add(a, b):
    return a + b

result = add(3, 5)
print(result)  # Output: 8
```

Default Parameters

You can define default values for function parameters. If a default parameter is not provided when the function is called, the default value is used.

```python
def greet(name="World"):
    print(f"Hello, {name}!")

greet()         # Output: Hello, World!
greet("Alice")  # Output: Hello, Alice!
```

Variable-Length Arguments

Python allows you to define functions that accept a variable number of arguments using `*args` for positional arguments and `**kwargs` for keyword arguments.

```python
def print_args(*args):
    for arg in args:
        print(arg)

print_args(1, 2, 3)  # Output: 1, 2, 3
```

```python
def print_kwargs(**kwargs):
    for key, value in kwargs.items():
        print(f"{key}: {value}")

print_kwargs(name="Alice", age=25)   # Output: name: Alice, age: 25
```

Modules

A module is a file containing Python code that can be imported and used in other Python programs. You can create your own modules by saving Python code in a `.py` file and importing it using the `import` statement.

Creating a Module

Create a file named `my_module.py` with the following content:

```python
# my_module.py
def add(a, b):
    return a + b

def subtract(a, b):
    return a - b
```

Importing a Module

You can import the module and use its functions in another Python file:

```python
# main.py
import my_module

result_add = my_module.add(3, 5)
result_subtract = my_module.subtract(10, 4)

print(result_add)          # Output: 8
print(result_subtract)     # Output: 6
```

Importing Specific Functions

You can also import specific functions from a module using the `from ... import ...` syntax:

```python
# main.py
from my_module import add

result = add(3, 5)
print(result)   # Output: 8
```

Organizing Code with Packages

Packages are collections of modules organized in directories. A package is identified by the presence of an `__init__.py` file in the directory. You can organize related modules into packages for better code organization.

Creating a Package

Create a directory structure like this:

```
my_package/
├── __init__.py
├── module1.py
├── module2.py
```

Using a Package

You can import modules from the package:

```python
# main.py
from my_package import module1, module2

result1 = module1.some_function()
result2 = module2.another_function()
```

Conclusion

Functions and modules are powerful tools for organizing and reusing code in Python. Functions allow you to encapsulate code into reusable blocks, while modules and packages enable you to structure your codebase efficiently. Understanding and using these concepts will help you create more maintainable and modular game code with PyGame.

Error Handling and Debugging

Error handling and debugging are crucial aspects of programming that help you identify, diagnose, and fix issues in your code. Python provides several mechanisms for handling errors and debugging code effectively. In this section, we will explore the basics of error handling and debugging in Python.

Exceptions and Error Handling

An exception is an event that disrupts the normal flow of a program. Python provides a way to handle exceptions using `try`, `except`, `else`, and `finally` blocks.

Try and Except

The `try` block contains the code that may raise an exception, and the `except` block contains the code to handle the exception.

```
try:
    result = 10 / 0
except ZeroDivisionError:
    print("Cannot divide by zero")
```

In this example, a `ZeroDivisionError` is raised when attempting to divide by zero. The `except` block catches the exception and prints an error message.

Else and Finally

The `else` block is executed if no exception is raised, and the `finally` block is executed regardless of whether an exception is raised.

```
try:
    result = 10 / 2
except ZeroDivisionError:
    print("Cannot divide by zero")
else:
    print("Division successful")
finally:
    print("Execution complete")

# Output:
# Division successful
# Execution complete
```

Custom Exceptions

You can define your own custom exceptions by creating a new class that inherits from the built-in `Exception` class.

```python
class CustomError(Exception):
    pass

try:
    raise CustomError("This is a custom error")
except CustomError as e:
    print(e)  # Output: This is a custom error
```

Debugging

Debugging is the process of identifying and fixing bugs in your code. Python provides several tools and techniques for debugging.

Print Statements

One of the simplest ways to debug code is by using print statements to inspect the values of variables and the flow of the program.

```python
def divide(a, b):
    print(f"a: {a}, b: {b}")
    return a / b

result = divide(10, 2)
print(result)  # Output: a: 10, b: 2, 5.0
```

Using a Debugger

A debugger allows you to execute code line by line, set breakpoints, and inspect variables. Most modern code editors and IDEs have built-in debuggers. For example, Visual Studio Code and PyCharm provide powerful debugging tools.

Logging

The `logging` module in Python provides a flexible way to log messages from your code. Logging is useful for debugging and monitoring your application in production.

```python
import logging
```

```python
logging.basicConfig(level=logging.DEBUG)

def divide(a, b):
    logging.debug(f"a: {a}, b: {b}")
    return a / b

result = divide(10, 2)
logging.info(f"Result: {result}")
```

Using Assertions

Assertions are used to check conditions that should always be true in your code. If an assertion fails, it raises an `AssertionError`.

```python
def divide(a, b):
    assert b != 0, "b cannot be zero"
    return a / b

result = divide(10, 2)
print(result)  # Output: 5.0
```

Conclusion

Error handling and debugging are essential skills for any programmer. By effectively handling exceptions and using debugging tools, you can identify and fix issues in your code more efficiently. These practices will help you create more robust and reliable games with PyGame.

Understanding these Python programming essentials will provide you with a strong foundation for developing games with PyGame. As you progress through this book, you will build on these fundamentals to create more complex and interactive games.

Chapter 3: Understanding PyGame Basics

Installing PyGame

Installing PyGame is the first step in creating games with Python. PyGame is a set of Python modules designed for writing video games. It includes computer graphics and sound libraries, allowing for the creation of complex games with ease.

To install PyGame, you can use the Python package manager `pip`. Open your command line interface and type the following command:

```
pip install pygame
```

This command will download and install the latest version of PyGame available. After the installation is complete, you can verify it by opening a Python interpreter and typing:

```
import pygame
print(pygame.__version__)
```

If the installation was successful, this will print the installed PyGame version.

It's important to ensure that your development environment is set up correctly. PyGame requires Python 3.6 or higher. You can download the latest version of Python from the official Python website. Additionally, make sure that `pip` is also installed and updated to the latest version.

In some cases, you might encounter issues during the installation, especially on Windows. Common issues include missing dependencies or permission errors. Ensure that your environment variables are correctly set up and that you have administrative rights.

If you are using an IDE like PyCharm or Visual Studio Code, you can also install PyGame directly through the IDE's package manager. For example, in PyCharm, you can go to `File -> Settings -> Project: [Your Project Name] -> Python Interpreter` and add `pygame` to the list of packages.

After installing PyGame, it's a good practice to create a virtual environment for your project. This helps manage dependencies and avoid conflicts between different projects. You can create a virtual environment using the following commands:

```
python -m venv myenv
source myenv/bin/activate # On Windows, use `myenv\Scripts\activate`
```

```
pip install pygame
```

Now that PyGame is installed and your environment is set up, you are ready to start creating games. The next steps will involve understanding the structure and components of PyGame, creating a basic game window, handling events, and drawing shapes and text on the screen.

PyGame Structure and Components

Understanding the structure and components of PyGame is crucial for effective game development. PyGame is built around the concept of a game loop, which continuously updates and renders the game state.

The main components of PyGame include:

1. **Display Surface**: The main display window where all game graphics are rendered. It is created using `pygame.display.set_mode((width, height))`.
2. **Game Clock**: Manages the frame rate of the game. It is controlled using `pygame.time.Clock()` and the `tick()` method.
3. **Events**: Handles user input and system events. Events are captured using `pygame.event.get()`.
4. **Sprites**: Represent game objects and characters. Sprites are managed using the `pygame.sprite.Sprite` class and `pygame.sprite.Group` for grouping multiple sprites.
5. **Sound and Music**: Manages sound effects and background music using `pygame.mixer`.

Here's an example of setting up a basic PyGame structure:

```
import pygame
import sys

# Initialize PyGame
pygame.init()

# Set up display
width, height = 800, 600
screen = pygame.display.set_mode((width, height))
pygame.display.set_caption("My PyGame Window")

# Set up game clock
clock = pygame.time.Clock()

# Main game loop
running = True
```

```
while running:
    for event in pygame.event.get():
        if event.type == pygame.QUIT:
            running = False

    # Clear screen
    screen.fill((0, 0, 0))

    # Update display
    pygame.display.flip()

    # Cap the frame rate
    clock.tick(60)

# Quit PyGame
pygame.quit()
sys.exit()
```

In this example, we initialize PyGame, set up the display surface, and enter the main game loop. The game loop handles events, updates the display, and maintains a consistent frame rate.

Each frame, the screen is cleared using `screen.fill((0, 0, 0))`, and `pygame.display.flip()` updates the display. The `clock.tick(60)` call ensures the game runs at 60 frames per second.

Understanding these components and their interactions is key to building complex games. The next sections will delve deeper into creating a game window, handling events, and rendering graphics.

Creating a Basic Game Window

Creating a basic game window is the foundation of any game. In PyGame, this involves initializing the library, setting up the display surface, and managing the main game loop.

First, initialize PyGame and set up the display surface:

```
import pygame
import sys

# Initialize PyGame
pygame.init()
```

```python
# Set up display
width, height = 800, 600
screen = pygame.display.set_mode((width, height))
pygame.display.set_caption("My First Game")
```

Here, `pygame.display.set_mode((width, height))` creates the game window with the specified width and height. `pygame.display.set_caption("My First Game")` sets the window title.

Next, set up the game clock to control the frame rate:

```python
# Set up game clock
clock = pygame.time.Clock()
```

The game clock ensures that the game runs at a consistent speed. Use `clock.tick(fps)` in the game loop to cap the frame rate.

Now, create the main game loop:

```python
# Main game loop
running = True
while running:
    for event in pygame.event.get():
        if event.type == pygame.QUIT:
            running = False

    # Clear screen
    screen.fill((255, 255, 255))

    # Update display
    pygame.display.flip()

    # Cap the frame rate
    clock.tick(60)

# Quit PyGame
pygame.quit()
sys.exit()
```

In this loop, `pygame.event.get()` captures all events. If the quit event (`pygame.QUIT`) is detected, the loop exits. The screen is cleared each frame using `screen.fill((255, 255, 255))`, and `pygame.display.flip()` updates the display.

You can enhance this basic window by adding more features, such as background images, text, or shapes. For example, to draw a rectangle:

```
# Draw a rectangle
pygame.draw.rect(screen, (0, 128, 255), pygame.Rect(30, 30, 60, 60))
```

This command draws a blue rectangle at position (30, 30) with a width and height of 60 pixels.

Creating a basic game window is the first step in game development. With this setup, you can start adding more elements to your game, such as handling user input and drawing game objects.

Handling Events in PyGame

Handling events is crucial in any game to manage user inputs and interactions. PyGame provides an event queue that captures all events, such as keyboard presses, mouse movements, and window actions.

The event queue is accessed using `pygame.event.get()`. Here's an example of handling basic events:

```
import pygame
import sys

# Initialize PyGame
pygame.init()

# Set up display
width, height = 800, 600
screen = pygame.display.set_mode((width, height))
pygame.display.set_caption("Event Handling")

# Set up game clock
clock = pygame.time.Clock()

# Main game loop
running = True
while running:
    for event in pygame.event.get():
```

```python
            if event.type == pygame.QUIT:
                running = False
            elif event.type == pygame.KEYDOWN:
                if event.key == pygame.K_ESCAPE:
                    running = False
                elif event.key == pygame.K_LEFT:
                    print("Left arrow key pressed")
                elif event.key == pygame.K_RIGHT:
                    print("Right arrow key pressed")
            elif event.type == pygame.MOUSEBUTTONDOWN:
                if event.button == 1:  # Left mouse button
                    print(f"Mouse clicked at {event.pos}")

    # Clear screen
    screen.fill((255, 255, 255))

    # Update display
    pygame.display.flip()

    # Cap the frame rate
    clock.tick(60)

# Quit PyGame
pygame.quit()
sys.exit()
```

In this example, we handle three types of events:

1. **QUIT Event**: Exits the game when the window close button is clicked.
2. **KEYDOWN Event**: Detects when a key is pressed. For example, pressing the ESC key exits the game, and pressing the left or right arrow keys prints a message.
3. **MOUSEBUTTONDOWN Event**: Detects mouse button clicks and prints the position of the click.

Handling events allows you to interact with the game. You can extend this by adding more complex interactions, such as character movement or game state changes.

For instance, to move a character with arrow keys:

```python
# Character position
x, y = width // 2, height // 2
speed = 5
```

```python
# Main game loop
running = True
while running:
    for event in pygame.event.get():
        if event.type == pygame.QUIT:
            running = False

    keys = pygame.key.get_pressed()
    if keys[pygame.K_LEFT]:
        x -= speed
    if keys[pygame.K_RIGHT]:
        x += speed
    if keys[pygame.K_UP]:
        y -= speed
    if keys[pygame.K_DOWN]:
        y += speed

    # Clear screen
    screen.fill((255, 255, 255))

    # Draw character
    pygame.draw.rect(screen, (0, 128, 255), pygame.Rect(x, y, 60, 60))

    # Update display
    pygame.display.flip()

    # Cap the frame rate
    clock.tick(60)

# Quit PyGame
pygame.quit()
sys.exit()
```

In this enhanced loop, `pygame.key.get_pressed()` checks the state of all keys, and the character's position is updated accordingly. This basic movement logic can be expanded to include more complex behaviors and interactions.

Drawing Shapes and Text

Chapter 3: Understanding PyGame Basics

Drawing shapes and text in PyGame is essential for creating visual elements in your game. PyGame provides various functions to draw basic shapes like rectangles, circles, and lines, as well as render text.

To draw shapes, use the drawing functions provided by PyGame's `pygame.draw` module. Here's an example of drawing different shapes:

```python
import pygame
import sys

# Initialize PyGame
pygame.init()

# Set up display
width, height = 800, 600
screen = pygame.display.set_mode((width, height))
pygame.display.set_caption("Drawing Shapes")

# Set up game clock
clock = pygame.time.Clock()

# Main game loop
running = True
while running:
    for event in pygame.event.get():
        if event.type == pygame.QUIT:
            running = False

    # Clear screen
    screen.fill((255, 255, 255))

    # Draw shapes
    pygame.draw.rect(screen, (0, 128, 255), pygame.Rect(30, 30, 60, 60))
    pygame.draw.circle(screen, (255, 0, 0), (200, 200), 40)
    pygame.draw.line(screen, (0, 255, 0), (300, 300), (400, 400), 5)

    # Update display
    pygame.display.flip()

    # Cap the frame rate
    clock.tick(60)
```

```
# Quit PyGame
pygame.quit()
sys.exit()
```

In this example, we draw a rectangle, a circle, and a line. The `pygame.draw.rect` function draws a rectangle, `pygame.draw.circle` draws a circle, and `pygame.draw.line` draws a line. Each function takes the display surface, color, and shape parameters.

To render text, use PyGame's font module. First, initialize a font object and then render the text onto a surface:

```
# Initialize font
pygame.font.init()
font = pygame.font.SysFont('Arial', 30)

# Render text
text_surface = font.render('Hello, PyGame!', True, (0, 0, 0))

# Draw text
screen.blit(text_surface, (100, 100))
```

In this example, `pygame.font.SysFont('Arial', 30)` creates a font object with Arial font and size 30. The `render` method creates a text surface with the specified text and color. Finally, `screen.blit` draws the text surface onto the display.

Combining shapes and text allows you to create more complex visuals. For instance, you can create a button with text:

```
# Draw button
button_rect = pygame.Rect(300, 250, 200, 50)
pygame.draw.rect(screen, (0, 128, 255), button_rect)
text_surface = font.render('Click Me', True, (255, 255, 255))
screen.blit(text_surface, (button_rect.x + 50, button_rect.y + 10))
```

This draws a button as a rectangle and places the text in the center. Handling click events on this button involves checking the mouse position:

```
for event in pygame.event.get():
```

```
    if event.type == pygame.QUIT:
        running = False
    elif event.type == pygame.MOUSEBUTTONDOWN:
        if event.button == 1:  # Left mouse button
            if button_rect.collidepoint(event.pos):
                print("Button clicked!")
```

Drawing shapes and text is a fundamental aspect of game development, enabling you to create interactive and visually appealing games. The next chapters will build on this by introducing game graphics and design principles.

Chapter 4: Game Graphics and Design

Introduction to Game Art and Design

Game art and design play a crucial role in creating an engaging and visually appealing game. This involves designing characters, environments, and interfaces that enhance the player's experience.

Game art can be categorized into several types:

1. **Concept Art**: Initial sketches and ideas that define the visual style and direction of the game.
2. **Sprites**: 2D images or animations representing characters, objects, and backgrounds.
3. **Textures**: Images applied to 3D models to give them detail and realism.
4. **User Interface (UI)**: Elements like buttons, menus, and icons that allow players to interact with the game.

Designing game art requires a combination of creativity and technical skills. Tools like Adobe Photoshop, Illustrator, and specialized software like Aseprite and Blender are commonly used.

When designing game art, consider the following principles:

1. **Consistency**: Maintain a cohesive art style throughout the game to ensure a unified visual experience.
2. **Clarity**: Ensure that game elements are easily distinguishable and understandable by the player.
3. **Emotion**: Use color, shapes, and animations to evoke emotions and enhance the storytelling.

Creating game art involves several stages:

1. **Conceptualization**: Generate ideas and create rough sketches to explore different visual directions.
2. **Design**: Develop detailed designs and choose the final art style.
3. **Production**: Create final assets, including sprites, backgrounds, and UI elements.
4. **Integration**: Implement the art assets into the game, ensuring they work well with the gameplay and mechanics.

For example, to create a simple character sprite:

1. **Sketch**: Draw a rough outline of the character.
2. **Design**: Refine the sketch, adding details and choosing colors.
3. **Pixel Art**: Create the final sprite using pixel art techniques, ensuring it looks good at the intended resolution.

Here's an example of a basic pixel art character:

```python
# Basic Pixel Art Character Example

import pygame
import sys

# Initialize PyGame
pygame.init()

# Set up display
width, height = 800, 600
screen = pygame.display.set_mode((width, height))
pygame.display.set_caption("Pixel Art Character")

# Load character sprite
character = pygame.image.load('character.png')

# Main game loop
running = True
while running:
    for event in pygame.event.get():
        if event.type == pygame.QUIT:
            running = False

    # Clear screen
    screen.fill((255, 255, 255))

    # Draw character
    screen.blit(character, (width//2, height//2))

    # Update display
    pygame.display.flip()

# Quit PyGame
pygame.quit()
sys.exit()
```

In this example, `character.png` is a pixel art image of the character. The `screen.blit` function draws the character sprite onto the screen at the specified position.

Game art and design are integral to creating a captivating game. By following design principles and using the right tools, you can create visually stunning games that engage and delight players.

Using Images and Sprites in PyGame

Using images and sprites is fundamental in creating visually engaging games. Sprites are 2D images or animations that represent characters, objects, and other elements in your game.

To use images in PyGame, you need to load and display them on the screen. PyGame provides functions to handle image loading, drawing, and manipulation.

First, load an image using `pygame.image.load`:

```python
import pygame
import sys

# Initialize PyGame
pygame.init()

# Set up display
width, height = 800, 600
screen = pygame.display.set_mode((width, height))
pygame.display.set_caption("Using Images")

# Load image
image = pygame.image.load('path/to/your/image.png')

# Main game loop
running = True
while running:
    for event in pygame.event.get():
        if event.type == pygame.QUIT:
            running = False

    # Clear screen
    screen.fill((255, 255, 255))

    # Draw image
    screen.blit(image, (100, 100))
```

```
    # Update display
    pygame.display.flip()

# Quit PyGame
pygame.quit()
sys.exit()
```

In this example, `pygame.image.load('path/to/your/image.png')` loads the image, and `screen.blit(image, (100, 100))` draws it at the specified position.

To create and manage sprites, PyGame provides the `pygame.sprite` module. Sprites are instances of the `pygame.sprite.Sprite` class, and they can be grouped using `pygame.sprite.Group`.

Here's an example of creating a sprite class and using a sprite group:

```
class Player(pygame.sprite.Sprite):
    def __init__(self):
        super().__init__()
        self.image = pygame.image.load('path/to/player/image.png')
        self.rect = self.image.get_rect()
        self.rect.center = (width // 2, height // 2)

# Initialize player sprite
player = Player()

# Create sprite group
all_sprites = pygame.sprite.Group()
all_sprites.add(player)

# Main game loop
running = True
while running:
    for event in pygame.event.get():
        if event.type == pygame.QUIT:
            running = False

    # Clear screen
    screen.fill((255, 255, 255))

    # Update and draw all sprites
```

```
    all_sprites.update()
    all_sprites.draw(screen)

    # Update display
    pygame.display.flip()

# Quit PyGame
pygame.quit()
sys.exit()
```

In this example, the `Player` class inherits from `pygame.sprite.Sprite` and initializes the player sprite. The `all_sprites` group manages all sprite instances, calling their `update` and `draw` methods each frame.

Sprites can also handle animations by updating their images or positions in the `update` method. For example, to animate a walking character:

```
class Player(pygame.sprite.Sprite):
    def __init__(self):
        super().__init__()
        self.images = [pygame.image.load(f'walk_{i}.png') for i in range(4)]
        self.index = 0
        self.image = self.images[self.index]
        self.rect = self.image.get_rect()
        self.rect.center = (width // 2, height // 2)

    def update(self):
        self.index += 1
        if self.index >= len(self.images):
            self.index = 0
        self.image = self.images[self.index]

# Initialize player sprite
player = Player()

# Create sprite group
all_sprites = pygame.sprite.Group()
all_sprites.add(player)

# Main game loop
```

```
running = True
while running:
    for event in pygame.event.get():
        if event.type == pygame.QUIT:
            running = False

    # Clear screen
    screen.fill((255, 255, 255))

    # Update and draw all sprites
    all_sprites.update()
    all_sprites.draw(screen)

    # Update display
    pygame.display.flip()

# Quit PyGame
pygame.quit()
sys.exit()
```

In this example, the `Player` class cycles through a list of images to create a walking animation. The `update` method increments the index and updates the sprite's image.

Using images and sprites effectively enhances the visual appeal and interactivity of your game. By leveraging PyGame's sprite management and animation capabilities, you can create dynamic and engaging game experiences.

Animating Sprites

Animating sprites is a crucial aspect of creating dynamic and engaging games. PyGame provides tools to handle sprite animations, allowing characters and objects to move and change their appearance over time.

To animate a sprite, you typically cycle through a series of images, creating the illusion of movement. Here's an example of a basic sprite animation:

```
import pygame
import sys

# Initialize PyGame
pygame.init()
```

```python
# Set up display
width, height = 800, 600
screen = pygame.display.set_mode((width, height))
pygame.display.set_caption("Animating Sprites")

class AnimatedSprite(pygame.sprite.Sprite):
    def __init__(self, images, pos):
        super().__init__()
        self.images = images
        self.index = 0
        self.image = self.images[self.index]
        self.rect = self.image.get_rect()
        self.rect.topleft = pos

    def update(self):
        self.index += 1
        if self.index >= len(self.images):
            self.index = 0
        self.image = self.images[self.index]

# Load images
images = [pygame.image.load(f'frame_{i}.png') for i in range(4)]

# Initialize animated sprite
animated_sprite = AnimatedSprite(images, (100, 100))

# Create sprite group
all_sprites = pygame.sprite.Group(animated_sprite)

# Main game loop
running = True
while running:
    for event in pygame.event.get():
        if event.type == pygame.QUIT:
            running = False

    # Clear screen
    screen.fill((255, 255, 255))

    # Update and draw all sprites
    all_sprites.update()
```

```
        all_sprites.draw(screen)

        # Update display
        pygame.display.flip()

# Quit PyGame
pygame.quit()
sys.exit()
```

In this example, the `AnimatedSprite` class cycles through a list of images (`frame_0.png`, `frame_1.png`, etc.) to create an animation. The `update` method increments the index and updates the sprite's image.

To control the speed of the animation, you can adjust the frame rate or add a delay between frame changes. Here's an example with a frame delay:

```
class AnimatedSprite(pygame.sprite.Sprite):
    def __init__(self, images, pos):
        super().__init__()
        self.images = images
        self.index = 0
        self.image = self.images[self.index]
        self.rect = self.image.get_rect()
        self.rect.topleft = pos
        self.animation_delay = 100  # milliseconds
        self.last_update = pygame.time.get_ticks()

    def update(self):
        now = pygame.time.get_ticks()
        if now - self.last_update > self.animation_delay:
            self.last_update = now
            self.index += 1
            if self.index >= len(self.images):
                self.index = 0
            self.image = self.images[self.index]

# Initialize animated sprite
animated_sprite = AnimatedSprite(images, (100, 100))
```

In this example, the `animation_delay` variable controls the time between frame changes, and `pygame.time.get_ticks()` is used to track time.

Animating sprites can also involve moving them across the screen. For example, to create a walking character:

```python
class Player(pygame.sprite.Sprite):
    def __init__(self, images, pos):
        super().__init__()
        self.images = images
        self.index = 0
        self.image = self.images[self.index]
        self.rect = self.image.get_rect()
        self.rect.topleft = pos
        self.animation_delay = 100
        self.last_update = pygame.time.get_ticks()
        self.velocity = 5

    def update(self):
        now = pygame.time.get_ticks()
        if now - self.last_update > self.animation_delay:
            self.last_update = now
            self.index += 1
            if self.index >= len(self.images):
                self.index = 0
            self.image = self.images[self.index]

        # Move the sprite
        keys = pygame.key.get_pressed()
        if keys[pygame.K_LEFT]:
            self.rect.x -= self.velocity
        if keys[pygame.K_RIGHT]:
            self.rect.x += self.velocity
        if keys[pygame.K_UP]:
            self.rect.y -= self.velocity
        if keys[pygame.K_DOWN]:
            self.rect.y += self.velocity

# Initialize player sprite
player = Player(images, (100, 100))
```

```python
# Create sprite group
all_sprites = pygame.sprite.Group(player)

# Main game loop
running = True
while running:
    for event in pygame.event.get():
        if event.type == pygame.QUIT:
            running = False

    # Clear screen
    screen.fill((255, 255, 255))

    # Update and draw all sprites
    all_sprites.update()
    all_sprites.draw(screen)

    # Update display
    pygame.display.flip()

# Quit PyGame
pygame.quit()
sys.exit()
```

In this example, the player sprite moves in response to arrow key presses while animating. The `update` method handles both animation and movement, creating a dynamic character.

Animating sprites adds life to your game, making it more engaging and visually appealing. By combining animation with user input and game logic, you can create rich and interactive game experiences.

Managing Sprite Groups

Managing sprite groups is essential for organizing and controlling multiple sprites in a game. PyGame provides the `pygame.sprite.Group` class, which allows you to group sprites together and perform operations on the entire group.

Sprite groups make it easier to update, draw, and manage collisions between multiple sprites. Here's an example of creating and managing a sprite group:

```python
import pygame
import sys
```

```python
# Initialize PyGame
pygame.init()

# Set up display
width, height = 800, 600
screen = pygame.display.set_mode((width, height))
pygame.display.set_caption("Sprite Groups")

class Player(pygame.sprite.Sprite):
    def __init__(self, image, pos):
        super().__init__()
        self.image = pygame.image.load(image)
        self.rect = self.image.get_rect()
        self.rect.topleft = pos

    def update(self):
        keys = pygame.key.get_pressed()
        if keys[pygame.K_LEFT]:
            self.rect.x -= 5
        if keys[pygame.K_RIGHT]:
            self.rect.x += 5
        if keys[pygame.K_UP]:
            self.rect.y -= 5
        if keys[pygame.K_DOWN]:
            self.rect.y += 5

# Initialize player sprite
player = Player('path/to/player/image.png', (100, 100))

# Create sprite group
all_sprites = pygame.sprite.Group()
all_sprites.add(player)

# Main game loop
running = True
while running:
    for event in pygame.event.get():
        if event.type == pygame.QUIT:
            running = False
```

```python
    # Clear screen
    screen.fill((255, 255, 255))

    # Update and draw all sprites
    all_sprites.update()
    all_sprites.draw(screen)

    # Update display
    pygame.display.flip()

# Quit PyGame
pygame.quit()
sys.exit()
```

In this example, the `Player` class defines a sprite that can move based on keyboard input. The player sprite is added to the `all_sprites` group, which manages all sprite updates and drawing.

You can add multiple sprites to a group and manage them collectively. For example, to create enemy sprites:

```python
class Enemy(pygame.sprite.Sprite):
    def __init__(self, image, pos):
        super().__init__()
        self.image = pygame.image.load(image)
        self.rect = self.image.get_rect()
        self.rect.topleft = pos

# Initialize enemy sprites
enemy1 = Enemy('path/to/enemy/image.png', (300, 200))
enemy2 = Enemy('path/to/enemy/image.png', (500, 400))

# Add enemies to the sprite group
all_sprites.add(enemy1, enemy2)
```

Now, the `all_sprites` group contains the player and enemies. The `update` and `draw` methods are called for all sprites in the group, ensuring they are all managed efficiently.

Sprite groups also support collision detection. For example, to check for collisions between the player and enemies:

```
# Check for collisions
collisions = pygame.sprite.spritecollide(player, all_sprites, False)
if collisions:
    print("Player collided with an enemy!")
```

The `pygame.sprite.spritecollide` function checks for collisions between a single sprite and a group of sprites. The `False` argument indicates that colliding sprites should not be removed from the group.

You can create multiple sprite groups for different purposes, such as separating players, enemies, and projectiles. For example:

```
# Create separate groups for players and enemies
players = pygame.sprite.Group(player)
enemies = pygame.sprite.Group(enemy1, enemy2)

# Update and draw all sprites
players.update()
enemies.update()
players.draw(screen)
enemies.draw(screen)
```

Managing sprite groups helps organize your game and improve performance by grouping related sprites together. This approach simplifies the code and allows for efficient updates and collision handling.

Designing Your Game's Visuals

Designing your game's visuals involves creating an aesthetically pleasing and cohesive look that enhances the gameplay experience. This includes everything from the game's overall art style to specific visual elements like characters, backgrounds, and user interfaces.

Art Style

Choosing an art style is the first step in designing your game's visuals. The art style sets the tone and atmosphere of the game. Common art styles include pixel art, cartoon, realistic, and minimalist. Consider your game's theme and target audience when selecting an art style.

Characters and Sprites

Character design is crucial as it defines the player's and NPCs' appearance. Create detailed and expressive characters that fit your game's theme. Use consistent colors, shapes, and animations to make characters recognizable and appealing.

Backgrounds and Environments

Designing backgrounds and environments involves creating the world in which your game takes place. Whether it's a lush forest, a bustling city, or an alien planet, the environment should immerse the player in the game world. Use layers to create depth and parallax scrolling to enhance the visual experience.

User Interface

The user interface (UI) includes menus, buttons, health bars, and other elements that allow players to interact with the game. A well-designed UI is intuitive and complements the game's art style. Ensure that the UI elements are clear and easily readable.

Visual Effects

Visual effects like particle systems, lighting, and shadows add dynamism and polish to your game. Use these effects to highlight important actions, create atmosphere, and make the game more visually engaging. However, use them sparingly to avoid overwhelming the player.

Color Scheme

Choosing a color scheme is essential for creating a cohesive visual experience. Use color theory to select complementary colors that enhance the game's mood and readability. Consistent use of colors helps players quickly identify different game elements.

Animation

Animation brings your game to life. Whether it's character movements, environmental animations, or UI transitions, smooth and expressive animations make the game more engaging. Pay attention to the timing and easing of animations to create a natural feel.

Consistency

Consistency is key to good visual design. Ensure that all visual elements follow the same style and quality. Inconsistent visuals can break immersion and confuse players. Create a style guide to maintain consistency across different assets.

Iteration

Designing visuals is an iterative process. Start with rough sketches and gradually refine them based on feedback and testing. Don't be afraid to make changes to improve the overall visual quality.

Tools

Use appropriate tools for creating game visuals. Popular tools include:

- **Adobe Photoshop**: For creating and editing images and textures.
- **Adobe Illustrator**: For vector graphics and UI elements.
- **Aseprite**: For pixel art and sprite animations.
- **Blender**: For 3D modeling and animations.
- **Tiled**: For designing tile-based game levels.

Example: Creating a Character Sprite

Here's an example of creating a simple character sprite using Aseprite:

1. **Sketch**: Start with a rough sketch of the character to define its shape and proportions.
2. **Outline**: Create a clean outline of the character using solid lines.
3. **Base Colors**: Fill the character with base colors, choosing a color palette that fits the game's theme.
4. **Shading**: Add shading and highlights to give the character depth and volume.
5. **Details**: Add details like facial features, clothing patterns, and accessories.
6. **Animation**: Create different frames for animations such as walking, jumping, and attacking.

Integrating Visuals into PyGame

Once you have your visual assets, integrate them into your PyGame project. Load images and sprites, set up backgrounds, and draw UI elements.

```
# Load and draw background
background = pygame.image.load('background.png')
screen.blit(background, (0, 0))

# Draw character sprite
player_image = pygame.image.load('player.png')
screen.blit(player_image, (player_x, player_y))

# Draw UI element
font = pygame.font.SysFont('Arial', 30)
score_text = font.render(f'Score: {score}', True, (255, 255, 255))
screen.blit(score_text, (10, 10))
```

In this example, the background image, character sprite, and score text are drawn onto the screen. Ensure that visual elements are properly layered and positioned to create a polished look.

Chapter 4: Game Graphics and Design

Designing your game's visuals is a critical aspect of game development. By following best practices and iterating on your designs, you can create a visually stunning game that captivates players and enhances the overall experience.

Chapter 5: Handling User Input

Keyboard Input

Handling keyboard input in PyGame is crucial for creating interactive games. By capturing and responding to key presses, you can control game elements like player movements, menu selections, and other interactions. PyGame provides robust methods to detect and handle keyboard events effectively.

To handle keyboard input, you need to use PyGame's event handling system. The `pygame.event.get()` function returns a list of all events that have occurred since the last call. By iterating through this list, you can check for specific event types and respond accordingly. Keyboard events are represented by `pygame.KEYDOWN` (when a key is pressed) and `pygame.KEYUP` (when a key is released).

Here's a basic example of handling keyboard input in PyGame:

```python
import pygame

# Initialize PyGame
pygame.init()

# Set up the display
screen = pygame.display.set_mode((800, 600))
pygame.display.set_caption('Keyboard Input Example')

# Main game loop
running = True
while running:
    for event in pygame.event.get():
        if event.type == pygame.QUIT:
            running = False
        elif event.type == pygame.KEYDOWN:
            if event.key == pygame.K_ESCAPE:
                running = False
            elif event.key == pygame.K_LEFT:
                print("Left arrow key pressed")
            elif event.key == pygame.K_RIGHT:
                print("Right arrow key pressed")

    # Update the display
```

```
    pygame.display.flip()

# Quit PyGame
pygame.quit()
```

In this example, the game loop continuously checks for events. When a `pygame.KEYDOWN` event is detected, the program checks which key was pressed using the `event.key` attribute. Specific actions are performed based on the key pressed, such as printing messages to the console.

To handle continuous key presses (holding down a key), you can use the `pygame.key.get_pressed()` function. This function returns a list of boolean values indicating the state of each key.

Here's an example:

```
import pygame

# Initialize PyGame
pygame.init()

# Set up the display
screen = pygame.display.set_mode((800, 600))
pygame.display.set_caption('Continuous Key Press Example')

# Main game loop
running = True
while running:
    for event in pygame.event.get():
        if event.type == pygame.QUIT:
            running = False

    keys = pygame.key.get_pressed()
    if keys[pygame.K_LEFT]:
        print("Left arrow key is being held down")
    if keys[pygame.K_RIGHT]:
        print("Right arrow key is being held down")

    # Update the display
    pygame.display.flip()
```

```python
# Quit PyGame
pygame.quit()
```

In this example, the `pygame.key.get_pressed()` function is used to check the state of the left and right arrow keys continuously. This allows the program to detect if a key is being held down, not just pressed once.

Handling keyboard input is not limited to directional controls. You can use any key on the keyboard to perform different actions in your game. PyGame supports a wide range of key constants, such as `pygame.K_SPACE` for the space bar, `pygame.K_RETURN` for the Enter key, and many others.

For more complex input handling, such as implementing key combinations or custom controls, you can create functions to manage these interactions. Here's an example of implementing a simple key combination:

```python
import pygame

# Initialize PyGame
pygame.init()

# Set up the display
screen = pygame.display.set_mode((800, 600))
pygame.display.set_caption('Key Combination Example')

# Function to check key combination
def check_key_combination():
    keys = pygame.key.get_pressed()
    if keys[pygame.K_LCTRL] and keys[pygame.K_c]:
        print("Ctrl+C combination pressed")

# Main game loop
running = True
while running:
    for event in pygame.event.get():
        if event.type == pygame.QUIT:
            running = False

    check_key_combination()

    # Update the display
    pygame.display.flip()
```

```
# Quit PyGame
pygame.quit()
```

In this example, the `check_key_combination()` function checks if both the left control key (`pygame.K_LCTRL`) and the 'C' key (`pygame.K_c`) are pressed simultaneously. If the combination is detected, a message is printed to the console.

By mastering keyboard input handling in PyGame, you can create more dynamic and interactive games, enhancing the player experience through responsive and intuitive controls.

Mouse Input

Handling mouse input in PyGame is essential for creating interactive and engaging games. By capturing and responding to mouse events, you can implement features like clicking on buttons, dragging objects, and more. PyGame provides various functions to detect and handle mouse events effectively.

Mouse events in PyGame are represented by `pygame.MOUSEBUTTONDOWN` (when a mouse button is pressed), `pygame.MOUSEBUTTONUP` (when a mouse button is released), and `pygame.MOUSEMOTION` (when the mouse is moved). You can use these events to interact with the game environment.

Here's a basic example of handling mouse input in PyGame:

```
import pygame

# Initialize PyGame
pygame.init()

# Set up the display
screen = pygame.display.set_mode((800, 600))
pygame.display.set_caption('Mouse Input Example')

# Main game loop
running = True
while running:
    for event in pygame.event.get():
        if event.type == pygame.QUIT:
            running = False
        elif event.type == pygame.MOUSEBUTTONDOWN:
```

```
            if event.button == 1:  # Left mouse button
                print("Left mouse button pressed at", event.pos)
            elif event.button == 3:  # Right mouse button
                print("Right mouse button pressed at", event.pos)
        elif event.type == pygame.MOUSEMOTION:
            print("Mouse moved to", event.pos)

    # Update the display
    pygame.display.flip()

# Quit PyGame
pygame.quit()
```

In this example, the game loop continuously checks for events. When a `pygame.MOUSEBUTTONDOWN` event is detected, the program checks which mouse button was pressed using the `event.button` attribute and prints the position of the click. The `pygame.MOUSEMOTION` event detects and prints the mouse's position as it moves.

To handle mouse clicks on specific objects, you can use the mouse position to check if it intersects with an object's bounding box. Here's an example of handling clicks on a rectangle:

```
import pygame

# Initialize PyGame
pygame.init()

# Set up the display
screen = pygame.display.set_mode((800, 600))
pygame.display.set_caption('Mouse Click on Rectangle')

# Define a rectangle
rect = pygame.Rect(100, 100, 200, 150)

# Main game loop
running = True
while running:
    for event in pygame.event.get():
        if event.type == pygame.QUIT:
            running = False
        elif event.type == pygame.MOUSEBUTTONDOWN:
```

```
                if event.button == 1:   # Left mouse button
                    if rect.collidepoint(event.pos):
                        print("Rectangle clicked!")

    # Clear the screen
    screen.fill((0, 0, 0))

    # Draw the rectangle
    pygame.draw.rect(screen, (255, 0, 0), rect)

    # Update the display
    pygame.display.flip()

# Quit PyGame
pygame.quit()
```

In this example, a rectangle is defined using `pygame.Rect`. The `collidepoint()` method checks if the mouse click position intersects with the rectangle's bounding box. If a collision is detected, a message is printed to the console.

Handling mouse input is not limited to clicks. You can also detect mouse wheel movements using the `pygame.MOUSEBUTTONDOWN` event with `event.button` values 4 and 5 for wheel up and wheel down, respectively. Here's an example:

```
import pygame

# Initialize PyGame
pygame.init()

# Set up the display
screen = pygame.display.set_mode((800, 600))
pygame.display.set_caption('Mouse Wheel Example')

# Main game loop
running = True
while running:
    for event in pygame.event.get():
        if event.type == pygame.QUIT:
            running = False
        elif event.type == pygame.MOUSEBUTTONDOWN:
            if event.button == 4:   # Mouse wheel up
```

```
            print("Mouse wheel scrolled up")
        elif event.button == 5:  # Mouse wheel down
            print("Mouse wheel scrolled down")

    # Update the display
    pygame.display.flip()

# Quit PyGame
pygame.quit()
```

In this example, mouse wheel movements are detected and corresponding messages are printed to the console.

By effectively handling mouse input, you can create more interactive and engaging games. Whether it's clicking on objects, dragging elements, or using the mouse wheel, mastering these interactions will enhance the overall user experience in your PyGame projects.

Joystick and Gamepad Input

Handling joystick and gamepad input in PyGame allows you to support various input devices, enhancing the gaming experience for players who prefer using controllers. PyGame provides robust support for joystick and gamepad input, making it easy to integrate these devices into your games.

To handle joystick and gamepad input, you first need to initialize the joystick module and detect connected devices. PyGame's `pygame.joystick` module provides functions to manage and read input from joysticks and gamepads.

Here's a basic example of initializing and detecting joysticks in PyGame:

```
import pygame

# Initialize PyGame
pygame.init()

# Initialize the joystick module
pygame.joystick.init()

# Get the number of joysticks connected
joystick_count = pygame.joystick.get_count()
print(f"Number of joysticks connected: {joystick_count}")

# Initialize each joystick
```

```
joysticks = []
for i in range(joystick_count):
    joystick = pygame.joystick.Joystick(i)
    joystick.init()
    joysticks.append(joystick)
    print(f"Joystick {i} initialized: {joystick.get_name()}")

# Main game loop
running = True
while running:
    for event in pygame.event.get():
        if event.type == pygame.QUIT:
            running = False

    # Update the display
    pygame.display.flip()

# Quit PyGame
pygame.quit()
```

In this example, the joystick module is initialized using `pygame.joystick.init()`. The `pygame.joystick.get_count()` function returns the number of connected joysticks. Each joystick is then initialized using `pygame.joystick.Joystick(i).init()`, and its name is printed.

To handle joystick input, you need to read the state of joystick buttons and axes. Joystick events are represented by `pygame.JOYBUTTONDOWN` (when a joystick button is pressed), `pygame.JOYBUTTONUP` (when a joystick button is released), and `pygame.JOYAXISMOTION` (when a joystick axis is moved).

Here's an example of handling joystick button and axis events:

```
import pygame

# Initialize PyGame
pygame.init()

# Initialize the joystick module
pygame.joystick.init()

# Initialize the first joystick
```

```python
joystick = pygame.joystick.Joystick(0)
joystick.init()

# Main game loop
running = True
while running:
    for event in pygame.event.get():
        if event.type == pygame.QUIT:
            running = False
        elif event.type == pygame.JOYBUTTONDOWN:
            print(f"Joystick button {event.button} pressed")
        elif event.type == pygame.JOYBUTTONUP:
            print(f"Joystick button {event.button} released")
        elif event.type == pygame.JOYAXISMOTION:
            print(f"Joystick axis {event.axis} moved to {event.value}")

    # Update the display
    pygame.display.flip()

# Quit PyGame
pygame.quit()
```

In this example, the game loop checks for joystick events. When a `pygame.JOYBUTTONDOWN` or `pygame.JOYBUTTONUP` event is detected, the program prints the button number. When a `pygame.JOYAXISMOTION` event is detected, the program prints the axis number and its new value.

You can also read the state of joystick buttons and axes continuously using the `get_button()` and `get_axis()` methods of the joystick object. Here's an example:

```python
import pygame

# Initialize PyGame
pygame.init()

# Initialize the joystick module
pygame.joystick.init()

# Initialize the first joystick
joystick = pygame.joystick.Joystick(0)
```

```
joystick.init()

# Main game loop
running = True
while running:
    for event in pygame.event.get():
        if event.type == pygame.QUIT:
            running = False

    # Read joystick button states
    for i in range(joystick.get_numbuttons()):
        if joystick.get_button(i):
            print(f"Joystick button {i} is pressed")

    # Read joystick axis states
    for i in range(joystick.get_numaxes()):
        axis_value = joystick.get_axis(i)
        print(f"Joystick axis {i} value: {axis_value}")

    # Update the display
    pygame.display.flip()

# Quit PyGame
pygame.quit()
```

In this example, the game loop continuously reads the state of all joystick buttons and axes. The `joystick.get_numbuttons()` and `joystick.get_numaxes()` methods return the number of buttons and axes on the joystick, respectively. The `joystick.get_button(i)` and `joystick.get_axis(i)` methods return the state of a specific button or axis.

By effectively handling joystick and gamepad input, you can create games that support a wide range of input devices, providing a more immersive and enjoyable experience for players. Whether it's button presses, axis movements, or custom controls, mastering joystick and gamepad input handling in PyGame is essential for modern game development.

Creating Custom Controls

Creating custom controls in PyGame allows you to design unique and intuitive input methods for your game. Custom controls can enhance the gameplay experience by providing players with tailored interactions that suit your game's mechanics. PyGame's flexible input handling system makes it easy to implement custom controls.

To create custom controls, you need to define how different inputs (keyboard, mouse, joystick) map to specific actions in your game. This involves detecting input events and responding with custom behaviors. Here's a step-by-step guide to creating custom controls in PyGame.

Step 1: Define Control Mappings

First, define a set of control mappings that associate specific inputs with game actions. For example, you might map the arrow keys to movement actions and the space bar to jumping.

```
controls = {
    "move_left": pygame.K_LEFT,
    "move_right": pygame.K_RIGHT,
    "jump": pygame.K_SPACE,
}
```

Step 2: Create a Control Handler

Next, create a control handler that checks for input events and triggers the corresponding actions. This involves iterating through the event queue and checking if any of the defined controls are activated.

```
def handle_controls(events):
    for event in events:
        if event.type == pygame.KEYDOWN:
            if event.key == controls["move_left"]:
                print("Move left")
            elif event.key == controls["move_right"]:
                print("Move right")
            elif event.key == controls["jump"]:
                print("Jump")
```

Step 3: Integrate Control Handler into Game Loop

Integrate the control handler into your game's main loop. Call the `handle_controls` function with the list of events to check for input and trigger the corresponding actions.

```
import pygame

# Initialize PyGame
```

```python
pygame.init()

# Set up the display
screen = pygame.display.set_mode((800, 600))
pygame.display.set_caption('Custom Controls Example')

# Define control mappings
controls = {
    "move_left": pygame.K_LEFT,
    "move_right": pygame.K_RIGHT,
    "jump": pygame.K_SPACE,
}

# Function to handle controls
def handle_controls(events):
    for event in events:
        if event.type == pygame.KEYDOWN:
            if event.key == controls["move_left"]:
                print("Move left")
            elif event.key == controls["move_right"]:
                print("Move right")
            elif event.key == controls["jump"]:
                print("Jump")

# Main game loop
running = True
while running:
    events = pygame.event.get()
    for event in events:
        if event.type == pygame.QUIT:
            running = False

    handle_controls(events)

    # Update the display
    pygame.display.flip()

# Quit PyGame
pygame.quit()
```

Step 4: Adding Mouse Controls

78 | Mastering Game Development With PyGame

You can extend the control handler to include mouse controls. For example, you might map a mouse button to a shooting action.

```
controls = {
    "move_left": pygame.K_LEFT,
    "move_right": pygame.K_RIGHT,
    "jump": pygame.K_SPACE,
    "shoot": pygame.BUTTON_LEFT,
}

def handle_controls(events):
    for event in events:
        if event.type == pygame.KEYDOWN:
            if event.key == controls["move_left"]:
                print("Move left")
            elif event.key == controls["move_right"]:
                print("Move right")
            elif event.key == controls["jump"]:
                print("Jump")
        elif event.type == pygame.MOUSEBUTTONDOWN:
            if event.button == controls["shoot"]:
                print("Shoot")
```

Step 5: Adding Joystick Controls

You can further extend the control handler to include joystick controls. Define mappings for joystick buttons and axes, and handle these inputs accordingly.

```
controls = {
    "move_left": pygame.K_LEFT,
    "move_right": pygame.K_RIGHT,
    "jump": pygame.K_SPACE,
    "shoot": pygame.BUTTON_LEFT,
    "joystick_move_left": (0, -1),   # Axis 0, negative direction
    "joystick_move_right": (0, 1),   # Axis 0, positive direction
}

def handle_controls(events):
    for event in events:
        if event.type == pygame.KEYDOWN:
```

```python
            if event.key == controls["move_left"]:
                print("Move left")
            elif event.key == controls["move_right"]:
                print("Move right")
            elif event.key == controls["jump"]:
                print("Jump")
        elif event.type == pygame.MOUSEBUTTONDOWN:
            if event.button == controls["shoot"]:
                print("Shoot")
        elif event.type == pygame.JOYAXISMOTION:
            if event.axis == controls["joystick_move_left"][0] and event.value < 0:
                print("Joystick move left")
            elif event.axis == controls["joystick_move_right"][0] and event.value > 0:
                print("Joystick move right")

# Initialize joystick
pygame.joystick.init()
joystick = pygame.joystick.Joystick(0)
joystick.init()
```

By following these steps, you can create custom controls that suit the unique mechanics and interactions of your game. Whether you're using the keyboard, mouse, or joystick, PyGame's flexible input handling system allows you to design intuitive and responsive controls for an enhanced gaming experience.

Managing Input Events

Managing input events effectively is crucial for creating a responsive and engaging game. PyGame provides a robust event handling system that allows you to manage various types of input events, including keyboard, mouse, and joystick inputs. By organizing and managing these events efficiently, you can create a smooth and intuitive gameplay experience.

Understanding the Event Queue

PyGame maintains an event queue that stores all input events generated by the user. You can access this queue using the `pygame.event.get()` function, which returns a list of all events that have occurred since the last call. By iterating through this list, you can process each event and respond accordingly.

Centralized Event Handling

To manage input events effectively, it's useful to create a centralized event handling system. This system can organize different types of input events and delegate them to appropriate handlers. Here's an example of a centralized event handling system:

```python
import pygame

# Initialize PyGame
pygame.init()

# Set up the display
screen = pygame.display.set_mode((800, 600))
pygame.display.set_caption('Centralized Event Handling Example')

# Event handlers
def handle_keydown(event):
    if event.key == pygame.K_LEFT:
        print("Left arrow key pressed")
    elif event.key == pygame.K_RIGHT:
        print("Right arrow key pressed")

def handle_mousebuttondown(event):
    if event.button == 1:  # Left mouse button
        print("Left mouse button pressed at", event.pos)
    elif event.button == 3:  # Right mouse button
        print("Right mouse button pressed at", event.pos)

def handle_joybuttondown(event):
    print(f"Joystick button {event.button} pressed")

# Main event handler
def handle_events(events):
    for event in events:
        if event.type == pygame.QUIT:
            return False
        elif event.type == pygame.KEYDOWN:
            handle_keydown(event)
        elif event.type == pygame.MOUSEBUTTONDOWN:
            handle_mousebuttondown(event)
        elif event.type == pygame.JOYBUTTONDOWN:
            handle_joybuttondown(event)
    return True
```

```python
# Initialize joystick
pygame.joystick.init()
if pygame.joystick.get_count() > 0:
    joystick = pygame.joystick.Joystick(0)
    joystick.init()

# Main game loop
running = True
while running:
    events = pygame.event.get()
    running = handle_events(events)

    # Update the display
    pygame.display.flip()

# Quit PyGame
pygame.quit()
```

In this example, separate functions handle different types of input events. The `handle_events` function processes the event queue and delegates events to the appropriate handlers. This centralized approach simplifies the management of input events and keeps the code organized.

Advanced Event Management

For more complex games, you might need advanced event management techniques, such as prioritizing events, managing multiple input sources, or creating custom event types. PyGame allows you to create custom events using the `pygame.event.Event` class and the `pygame.event.post` function.

Here's an example of creating and posting a custom event:

```python
import pygame

# Initialize PyGame
pygame.init()

# Define custom event type
CUSTOM_EVENT = pygame.USEREVENT + 1

# Create and post custom event
```

```
custom_event    =    pygame.event.Event(CUSTOM_EVENT,    message="Hello,
PyGame!")
pygame.event.post(custom_event)

# Main game loop
running = True
while running:
    for event in pygame.event.get():
        if event.type == pygame.QUIT:
            running = False
        elif event.type == CUSTOM_EVENT:
            print(event.message)

    # Update the display
    pygame.display.flip()

# Quit PyGame
pygame.quit()
```

In this example, a custom event type is defined using `pygame.USEREVENT + 1`. A custom event is created with a message attribute and posted to the event queue using `pygame.event.post`. The main game loop processes the custom event and prints the message.

Managing Multiple Input Sources

If your game supports multiple input sources (keyboard, mouse, joystick), it's important to manage these sources effectively. You can create a unified input manager that handles different input sources and maps them to game actions.

Here's an example of a unified input manager:

```
import pygame

# Initialize PyGame
pygame.init()

# Set up the display
screen = pygame.display.set_mode((800, 600))
pygame.display.set_caption('Unified Input Manager Example')

# Define control mappings
```

```python
controls = {
    "move_left": [pygame.K_LEFT, (0, -1)],   # Keyboard and joystick axis
    "move_right": [pygame.K_RIGHT, (0, 1)],
    "jump": [pygame.K_SPACE, None],  # Keyboard only
}

# Function to handle controls
def handle_controls(events):
    for event in events:
        if event.type == pygame.KEYDOWN:
            if event.key in controls["move_left"]:
                print("Move left")
            elif event.key in controls["move_right"]:
                print("Move right")
            elif event.key in controls["jump"]:
                print("Jump")
        elif event.type == pygame.JOYAXISMOTION:
            if   event.axis  ==  controls["move_left"][1][0]  and event.value < 0:
                print("Joystick move left")
            elif   event.axis  ==  controls["move_right"][1][0]  and event.value > 0:
                print("Joystick move right")

# Initialize joystick
pygame.joystick.init()
if pygame.joystick.get_count() > 0:
    joystick = pygame.joystick.Joystick(0)
    joystick.init()

# Main game loop
running = True
while running:
    events = pygame.event.get()
    for event in events:
        if event.type == pygame.QUIT:
            running = False

    handle_controls(events)
```

```
    # Update the display
    pygame.display.flip()

# Quit PyGame
pygame.quit()
```

In this example, control mappings are defined for both keyboard and joystick inputs. The `handle_controls` function checks for both types of inputs and triggers the corresponding actions.

By effectively managing input events, you can create a responsive and intuitive game that handles various input sources seamlessly. Whether you're dealing with simple keyboard input or complex combinations of keyboard, mouse, and joystick inputs, PyGame provides the tools you need to create a smooth and enjoyable gameplay experience.

Chapter 6: Sound and Music in Games

Adding Sound Effects

Adding sound effects to your game can significantly enhance the player experience by providing audio feedback for actions and events. PyGame's mixer module makes it easy to load and play sound effects, allowing you to create an immersive audio environment.

Initializing the Mixer

Before you can add sound effects, you need to initialize the mixer module. This is typically done at the beginning of your program, after initializing PyGame.

```
import pygame

# Initialize PyGame
pygame.init()

# Initialize the mixer
pygame.mixer.init()
```

Loading Sound Effects

Sound effects are typically stored as audio files (e.g., WAV, MP3). You can load these files into PyGame using the `pygame.mixer.Sound` class. Here's an example of loading a sound effect:

```
# Load a sound effect
jump_sound = pygame.mixer.Sound('jump.wav')
```

Playing Sound Effects

Once a sound effect is loaded, you can play it using the `play()` method. Here's an example of playing a sound effect when a key is pressed:

```
import pygame

# Initialize PyGame and the mixer
pygame.init()
```

```python
pygame.mixer.init()

# Load a sound effect
jump_sound = pygame.mixer.Sound('jump.wav')

# Set up the display
screen = pygame.display.set_mode((800, 600))
pygame.display.set_caption('Sound Effects Example')

# Main game loop
running = True
while running:
    for event in pygame.event.get():
        if event.type == pygame.QUIT:
            running = False
        elif event.type == pygame.KEYDOWN:
            if event.key == pygame.K_SPACE:
                jump_sound.play()  # Play the sound effect

    # Update the display
    pygame.display.flip()

# Quit PyGame
pygame.quit()
```

In this example, the `jump_sound.play()` method is called when the space bar is pressed, playing the sound effect.

Controlling Sound Playback

PyGame provides various methods to control sound playback, including stopping, pausing, and setting the volume. Here's an overview of some useful methods:

- `play()`: Plays the sound.
- `stop()`: Stops the sound.
- `fadeout(time)`: Fades out the sound over the specified time (in milliseconds).
- `set_volume(volume)`: Sets the volume of the sound (0.0 to 1.0).

Here's an example of controlling sound playback:

```
import pygame
```

Chapter 6: Sound and Music in Games

```python
# Initialize PyGame and the mixer
pygame.init()
pygame.mixer.init()

# Load a sound effect
jump_sound = pygame.mixer.Sound('jump.wav')

# Set up the display
screen = pygame.display.set_mode((800, 600))
pygame.display.set_caption('Sound Playback Control Example')

# Main game loop
running = True
while running:
    for event in pygame.event.get():
        if event.type == pygame.QUIT:
            running = False
        elif event.type == pygame.KEYDOWN:
            if event.key == pygame.K_SPACE:
                jump_sound.play()   # Play the sound effect
            elif event.key == pygame.K_s:
                jump_sound.stop()   # Stop the sound effect
            elif event.key == pygame.K_f:
                jump_sound.fadeout(1000)    # Fade out the sound effect over 1 second
            elif event.key == pygame.K_UP:
                jump_sound.set_volume(min(jump_sound.get_volume() + 0.1, 1.0))  # Increase volume
            elif event.key == pygame.K_DOWN:
                jump_sound.set_volume(max(jump_sound.get_volume() - 0.1, 0.0))  # Decrease volume

    # Update the display
    pygame.display.flip()

# Quit PyGame
pygame.quit()
```

In this example, additional keys are used to stop, fade out, and adjust the volume of the sound effect.

Using Multiple Sound Channels

PyGame's mixer module supports multiple sound channels, allowing you to play multiple sounds simultaneously. By default, PyGame uses a single channel, but you can specify additional channels if needed.

Here's an example of using multiple sound channels:

```python
import pygame

# Initialize PyGame and the mixer
pygame.init()
pygame.mixer.init()

# Set the number of channels
pygame.mixer.set_num_channels(8)

# Load sound effects
jump_sound = pygame.mixer.Sound('jump.wav')
shoot_sound = pygame.mixer.Sound('shoot.wav')

# Set up the display
screen = pygame.display.set_mode((800, 600))
pygame.display.set_caption('Multiple Sound Channels Example')

# Main game loop
running = True
while running:
    for event in pygame.event.get():
        if event.type == pygame.QUIT:
            running = False
        elif event.type == pygame.KEYDOWN:
            if event.key == pygame.K_SPACE:
                pygame.mixer.Channel(0).play(jump_sound)    # Play sound on channel 0
            elif event.key == pygame.K_s:
                pygame.mixer.Channel(1).play(shoot_sound)    # Play sound on channel 1

    # Update the display
    pygame.display.flip()
```

```python
# Quit PyGame
pygame.quit()
```

In this example, the jump sound is played on channel 0, and the shoot sound is played on channel 1. By using multiple channels, you can manage and control different sound effects independently.

Adding sound effects to your game can greatly enhance the player's experience by providing auditory feedback and creating a more immersive environment. By mastering PyGame's mixer module, you can effectively incorporate a wide range of sound effects into your games.

Incorporating Background Music

Incorporating background music into your game can significantly enhance the atmosphere and overall player experience. PyGame's mixer module provides the tools needed to load and play background music seamlessly.

Loading Background Music

Background music is typically stored as audio files (e.g., MP3, OGG). You can load these files using the `pygame.mixer.music` module. Here's an example of loading background music:

```python
import pygame

# Initialize PyGame and the mixer
pygame.init()
pygame.mixer.init()

# Load background music
pygame.mixer.music.load('background.mp3')
```

Playing Background Music

Once the music is loaded, you can play it using the `pygame.mixer.music.play()` method. Here's an example of playing background music:

```python
import pygame

# Initialize PyGame and the mixer
```

```python
pygame.init()
pygame.mixer.init()

# Load and play background music
pygame.mixer.music.load('background.mp3')
pygame.mixer.music.play(-1)    # -1 means the music will loop indefinitely

# Set up the display
screen = pygame.display.set_mode((800, 600))
pygame.display.set_caption('Background Music Example')

# Main game loop
running = True
while running:
    for event in pygame.event.get():
        if event.type == pygame.QUIT:
            running = False

    # Update the display
    pygame.display.flip()

# Quit PyGame
pygame.quit()
```

In this example, the `pygame.mixer.music.play(-1)` method is used to play the background music indefinitely. The argument `-1` specifies that the music should loop indefinitely.

Controlling Music Playback

PyGame provides various methods to control music playback, including pausing, stopping, and setting the volume. Here's an overview of some useful methods:

- `play(loops=0, start=0.0)`: Plays the music, with optional looping and start position.
- `stop()`: Stops the music.
- `pause()`: Pauses the music.
- `unpause()`: Resumes the music.
- `fadeout(time)`: Fades out the music over the specified time (in milliseconds).
- `set_volume(volume)`: Sets the volume of the music (0.0 to 1.0).

Here's an example of controlling music playback:

```python
import pygame

# Initialize PyGame and the mixer
pygame.init()
pygame.mixer.init()

# Load background music
pygame.mixer.music.load('background.mp3')

# Set up the display
screen = pygame.display.set_mode((800, 600))
pygame.display.set_caption('Music Playback Control Example')

# Main game loop
running = True
while running:
    for event in pygame.event.get():
        if event.type == pygame.QUIT:
            running = False
        elif event.type == pygame.KEYDOWN:
            if event.key == pygame.K_p:
                pygame.mixer.music.play(-1)  # Play the music
            elif event.key == pygame.K_s:
                pygame.mixer.music.stop()  # Stop the music
            elif event.key == pygame.K_a:
                pygame.mixer.music.pause()  # Pause the music
            elif event.key == pygame.K_u:
                pygame.mixer.music.unpause()  # Unpause the music
            elif event.key == pygame.K_f:
                pygame.mixer.music.fadeout(1000)   # Fade out the music over 1 second
            elif event.key == pygame.K_UP:
                volume = min(pygame.mixer.music.get_volume() + 0.1, 1.0)
                pygame.mixer.music.set_volume(volume)   # Increase volume
            elif event.key == pygame.K_DOWN:
                volume = max(pygame.mixer.music.get_volume() - 0.1, 0.0)
```

```
                    pygame.mixer.music.set_volume(volume)        #   Decrease
volume

    # Update the display
    pygame.display.flip()

# Quit PyGame
pygame.quit()
```

In this example, additional keys are used to control the playback of the background music, including playing, stopping, pausing, unpausing, fading out, and adjusting the volume.

Using Multiple Music Tracks

You can switch between different background music tracks by loading new audio files and playing them as needed. Here's an example of switching between two music tracks:

```
import pygame

# Initialize PyGame and the mixer
pygame.init()
pygame.mixer.init()

# Load music tracks
track1 = 'background1.mp3'
track2 = 'background2.mp3'

# Set up the display
screen = pygame.display.set_mode((800, 600))
pygame.display.set_caption('Multiple Music Tracks Example')

# Main game loop
running = True
current_track = track1
pygame.mixer.music.load(current_track)
pygame.mixer.music.play(-1)

while running:
    for event in pygame.event.get():
        if event.type == pygame.QUIT:
            running = False
```

```
        elif event.type == pygame.KEYDOWN:
            if event.key == pygame.K_1:
                current_track = track1
                pygame.mixer.music.load(current_track)
                pygame.mixer.music.play(-1)
            elif event.key == pygame.K_2:
                current_track = track2
                pygame.mixer.music.load(current_track)
                pygame.mixer.music.play(-1)

    # Update the display
    pygame.display.flip()

# Quit PyGame
pygame.quit()
```

In this example, pressing the '1' key loads and plays the first music track, while pressing the '2' key loads and plays the second music track.

By incorporating background music into your game, you can create a more immersive and engaging experience for players. Whether it's a looping track or dynamic music that changes based on game events, PyGame's mixer module provides the tools you need to enhance your game's audio environment.

Managing Sound Channels

Managing sound channels in PyGame is essential for controlling multiple sound effects and music tracks simultaneously. PyGame's mixer module allows you to allocate and manage multiple channels, giving you fine-grained control over audio playback.

Understanding Sound Channels

A sound channel in PyGame represents a virtual audio output. By default, PyGame uses a single channel for all sound effects, but you can create and manage additional channels to play multiple sounds simultaneously. Each channel can be controlled independently, allowing you to start, stop, pause, and adjust the volume of individual sounds.

Setting Up Sound Channels

To set up additional sound channels, you can use the `pygame.mixer.set_num_channels()` function. This function specifies the total number of sound channels available.

Here's an example of setting up eight sound channels:

```python
import pygame

# Initialize PyGame and the mixer
pygame.init()
pygame.mixer.init()

# Set the number of channels
pygame.mixer.set_num_channels(8)
```

Playing Sounds on Specific Channels

You can play a sound on a specific channel using the `pygame.mixer.Channel` class. The `Channel` class provides methods to control playback, such as `play()`, `stop()`, `pause()`, and `set_volume()`.

Here's an example of playing sounds on specific channels:

```python
import pygame

# Initialize PyGame and the mixer
pygame.init()
pygame.mixer.init()

# Set the number of channels
pygame.mixer.set_num_channels(8)

# Load sound effects
sound1 = pygame.mixer.Sound('sound1.wav')
sound2 = pygame.mixer.Sound('sound2.wav')

# Set up the display
screen = pygame.display.set_mode((800, 600))
pygame.display.set_caption('Sound Channels Example')

# Main game loop
running = True
while running:
    for event in pygame.event.get():
        if event.type == pygame.QUIT:
            running = False
```

```
            elif event.type == pygame.KEYDOWN:
                if event.key == pygame.K_1:
                    pygame.mixer.Channel(0).play(sound1)   # Play sound1
on channel 0
                elif event.key == pygame.K_2:
                    pygame.mixer.Channel(1).play(sound2)   # Play sound2
on channel 1

    # Update the display
    pygame.display.flip()

# Quit PyGame
pygame.quit()
```

In this example, pressing the '1' key plays `sound1` on channel 0, and pressing the '2' key plays `sound2` on channel 1. By using specific channels, you can control each sound independently.

Controlling Sound Channels

The `Channel` class provides various methods to control sound playback on specific channels. Here's an overview of some useful methods:

- `play(sound, loops=0, maxtime=0, fade_ms=0)`: Plays the specified sound on the channel.
- `stop()`: Stops the sound playing on the channel.
- `pause()`: Pauses the sound playing on the channel.
- `unpause()`: Resumes the paused sound on the channel.
- `set_volume(volume)`: Sets the volume of the channel (0.0 to 1.0).
- `get_busy()`: Returns `True` if the channel is currently playing a sound.

Here's an example of controlling sound playback on specific channels:

```
import pygame

# Initialize PyGame and the mixer
pygame.init()
pygame.mixer.init()

# Set the number of channels
pygame.mixer.set_num_channels(8)
```

```python
# Load sound effects
sound1 = pygame.mixer.Sound('sound1.wav')
sound2 = pygame.mixer.Sound('sound2.wav')

# Set up the display
screen = pygame.display.set_mode((800, 600))
pygame.display.set_caption('Channel Control Example')

# Main game loop
running = True
while running:
    for event in pygame.event.get():
        if event.type == pygame.QUIT:
            running = False
        elif event.type == pygame.KEYDOWN:
            if event.key == pygame.K_1:
                pygame.mixer.Channel(0).play(sound1)   # Play sound1 on channel 0
            elif event.key == pygame.K_2:
                pygame.mixer.Channel(1).play(sound2)   # Play sound2 on channel 1
            elif event.key == pygame.K_s:
                pygame.mixer.Channel(0).stop()   # Stop the sound on channel 0
            elif event.key == pygame.K_p:
                pygame.mixer.Channel(0).pause()   # Pause the sound on channel 0
            elif event.key == pygame.K_u:
                pygame.mixer.Channel(0).unpause()   # Unpause the sound on channel 0
            elif event.key == pygame.K_UP:
                volume = min(pygame.mixer.Channel(0).get_volume() + 0.1, 1.0)
                pygame.mixer.Channel(0).set_volume(volume)   # Increase volume on channel 0
            elif event.key == pygame.K_DOWN:
                volume = max(pygame.mixer.Channel(0).get_volume() - 0.1, 0.0)
                pygame.mixer.Channel(0).set_volume(volume)   # Decrease volume on channel 0
```

```
        # Update the display
        pygame.display.flip()

# Quit PyGame
pygame.quit()
```

In this example, additional keys are used to stop, pause, unpause, and adjust the volume of the sound playing on channel 0.

Using Channel Reservations

You can reserve specific channels for certain sounds, ensuring that they always play on the same channel. This is useful for managing important sounds that should not be interrupted.

Here's an example of reserving channels:

```
import pygame

# Initialize PyGame and the mixer
pygame.init()
pygame.mixer.init()

# Reserve the first two channels
pygame.mixer.set_reserved(2)

# Load sound effects
important_sound = pygame.mixer.Sound('important.wav')
regular_sound = pygame.mixer.Sound('regular.wav')

# Set up the display
screen = pygame.display.set_mode((800, 600))
pygame.display.set_caption('Reserved Channels Example')

# Main game loop
running = True
while running:
    for event in pygame.event.get():
        if event.type == pygame.QUIT:
            running = False
        elif event.type == pygame.KEYDOWN:
            if event.key == pygame.K_i:
```

```
                pygame.mixer.Channel(0).play(important_sound)        #
Play important sound on reserved channel 0
            elif event.key == pygame.K_r:
                pygame.mixer.Channel(2).play(regular_sound)    # Play
regular sound on channel 2

    # Update the display
    pygame.display.flip()

# Quit PyGame
pygame.quit()
```

In this example, the first two channels are reserved using `pygame.mixer.set_reserved(2)`. The important sound is always played on channel 0, ensuring it is not interrupted by other sounds.

By managing sound channels effectively, you can control multiple audio sources in your game, creating a richer and more immersive audio experience. Whether it's playing simultaneous sound effects or managing background music, PyGame's mixer module provides the tools you need to handle sound channels with precision.

Using Third-Party Sound Libraries

Using third-party sound libraries can enhance the audio capabilities of your PyGame projects by providing additional features and higher quality audio processing. Several libraries integrate well with PyGame, offering advanced sound manipulation and playback options.

Overview of Popular Libraries

1. **Pyglet**: A cross-platform windowing and multimedia library for Python, pyglet provides powerful audio capabilities and integrates well with OpenGL.
2. **PyAudio**: A set of Python bindings for PortAudio, PyAudio allows you to play and record audio streams.
3. **SoundFile**: A library for reading and writing sound files, SoundFile provides support for various audio formats and high-quality audio processing.

Integrating Pyglet with PyGame

Pyglet provides robust audio playback capabilities and can be integrated with PyGame for enhanced sound features. Here's an example of using Pyglet for audio playback in a PyGame project:

```
import pygame
import pyglet
```

```python
# Initialize PyGame
pygame.init()

# Set up the display
screen = pygame.display.set_mode((800, 600))
pygame.display.set_caption('Pyglet Audio Integration Example')

# Load and play a sound using Pyglet
sound = pyglet.media.load('sound.mp3', streaming=False)
sound.play()

# Main game loop
running = True
while running:
    for event in pygame.event.get():
        if event.type == pygame.QUIT:
            running = False

    # Update the display
    pygame.display.flip()

# Quit PyGame
pygame.quit()
```

In this example, Pyglet is used to load and play a sound file. The sound plays independently while the PyGame window is open.

Integrating PyAudio with PyGame

PyAudio allows you to play and record audio streams, providing low-level control over audio input and output. Here's an example of playing audio using PyAudio in a PyGame project:

```python
import pygame
import pyaudio
import wave

# Initialize PyGame
pygame.init()

# Set up the display
```

```python
screen = pygame.display.set_mode((800, 600))
pygame.display.set_caption('PyAudio Integration Example')

# Load and play a sound using PyAudio
filename = 'sound.wav'
wf = wave.open(filename, 'rb')

p = pyaudio.PyAudio()

# Open stream
stream = p.open(format=p.get_format_from_width(wf.getsampwidth()),
                channels=wf.getnchannels(),
                rate=wf.getframerate(),
                output=True)

# Read data
data = wf.readframes(1024)

# Main game loop
running = True
while running:
    for event in pygame.event.get():
        if event.type == pygame.QUIT:
            running = False

    # Play stream
    while len(data) > 0:
        stream.write(data)
        data = wf.readframes(1024)

    # Update the display
    pygame.display.flip()

# Stop stream
stream.stop_stream()
stream.close()

# Close PyAudio
p.terminate()

# Quit PyGame
```

```
pygame.quit()
```

In this example, PyAudio is used to play a WAV file. The audio stream is read and played in chunks, allowing for real-time audio playback.

Integrating SoundFile with PyGame

SoundFile provides high-quality audio processing and supports various audio formats. Here's an example of reading and playing audio using SoundFile in a PyGame project:

```
import pygame
import soundfile as sf
import numpy as np

# Initialize PyGame
pygame.init()

# Set up the display
screen = pygame.display.set_mode((800, 600))
pygame.display.set_caption('SoundFile Integration Example')

# Load a sound file using SoundFile
data, samplerate = sf.read('sound.wav')

# Convert the data to 16-bit integers
data = (data * 32767).astype(np.int16)

# Initialize PyGame mixer with the same sample rate
pygame.mixer.init(frequency=samplerate)

# Create a sound buffer from the data
sound = pygame.sndarray.make_sound(data)

# Play the sound
sound.play()

# Main game loop
running = True
while running:
    for event in pygame.event.get():
        if event.type == pygame.QUIT:
```

```
            running = False

    # Update the display
    pygame.display.flip()

# Quit PyGame
pygame.quit()
```

In this example, SoundFile is used to read a WAV file. The audio data is converted to 16-bit integers and played using PyGame's mixer.

By integrating third-party sound libraries, you can enhance the audio capabilities of your PyGame projects, offering advanced sound manipulation and high-quality audio processing. Whether it's using Pyglet for powerful audio playback, PyAudio for low-level audio control, or SoundFile for high-quality audio processing, these libraries provide the tools you need to create an immersive audio experience in your games.

Optimizing Audio for Performance

Optimizing audio for performance is crucial in game development to ensure smooth and responsive gameplay. PyGame's mixer module provides various tools and techniques to optimize audio playback and reduce latency.

Reducing Audio Latency

Audio latency is the delay between the time a sound is triggered and when it is heard. Reducing latency is important for creating responsive audio feedback. You can adjust the buffer size when initializing the mixer to reduce latency.

Here's an example of initializing the mixer with a smaller buffer size:

```
import pygame

# Initialize PyGame
pygame.init()

# Initialize the mixer with a smaller buffer size
pygame.mixer.init(buffer=512)

# Set up the display
screen = pygame.display.set_mode((800, 600))
pygame.display.set_caption('Audio Latency Optimization Example')
```

```python
# Main game loop
running = True
while running:
    for event in pygame.event.get():
        if event.type == pygame.QUIT:
            running = False

    # Update the display
    pygame.display.flip()

# Quit PyGame
pygame.quit()
```

In this example, the mixer is initialized with a buffer size of 512, reducing audio latency.

Preloading Sounds

Preloading sounds can help reduce latency by ensuring that audio files are loaded into memory before they are needed. This avoids delays caused by loading files during gameplay.

Here's an example of preloading sounds:

```python
import pygame

# Initialize PyGame and the mixer
pygame.init()
pygame.mixer.init()

# Preload sounds
jump_sound = pygame.mixer.Sound('jump.wav')
shoot_sound = pygame.mixer.Sound('shoot.wav')

# Set up the display
screen = pygame.display.set_mode((800, 600))
pygame.display.set_caption('Preloading Sounds Example')

# Main game loop
running = True
while running:
    for event in pygame.event.get():
        if event.type == pygame.QUIT:
```

```
            running = False
        elif event.type == pygame.KEYDOWN:
            if event.key == pygame.K_SPACE:
                jump_sound.play()  # Play preloaded sound
            elif event.key == pygame.K_s:
                shoot_sound.play()  # Play preloaded sound

    # Update the display
    pygame.display.flip()

# Quit PyGame
pygame.quit()
```

In this example, the `jump_sound` and `shoot_sound` files are preloaded into memory, reducing latency when they are played during gameplay.

Using Audio Formats Efficiently

Choosing the right audio format can impact performance. Uncompressed formats like WAV provide high quality but can be large in size. Compressed formats like OGG or MP3 are smaller but may require more processing power to decode.

Here's an example of using an OGG file for background music:

```
import pygame

# Initialize PyGame and the mixer
pygame.init()
pygame.mixer.init()

# Load and play background music (OGG format)
pygame.mixer.music.load('background.ogg')
pygame.mixer.music.play(-1)

# Set up the display
screen = pygame.display.set_mode((800, 600))
pygame.display.set_caption('Efficient Audio Format Example')

# Main game loop
running = True
while running:
    for event in pygame.event.get():
```

```
        if event.type == pygame.QUIT:
            running = False

    # Update the display
    pygame.display.flip()

# Quit PyGame
pygame.quit()
```

In this example, an OGG file is used for background music, balancing file size and quality.

Managing Sound Channels Efficiently

Efficiently managing sound channels can improve performance by avoiding unnecessary playback and reducing CPU usage. Only allocate channels for critical sounds and reuse channels when possible.

Here's an example of managing sound channels efficiently:

```
import pygame

# Initialize PyGame and the mixer
pygame.init()
pygame.mixer.init()

# Set the number of channels
pygame.mixer.set_num_channels(8)

# Load sound effects
jump_sound = pygame.mixer.Sound('jump.wav')
shoot_sound = pygame.mixer.Sound('shoot.wav')

# Set up the display
screen = pygame.display.set_mode((800, 600))
pygame.display.set_caption('Efficient Sound Channel Management Example')

# Main game loop
running = True
while running:
    for event in pygame.event.get():
        if event.type == pygame.QUIT:
```

```
            running = False
        elif event.type == pygame.KEYDOWN:
            if event.key == pygame.K_SPACE:
                pygame.mixer.find_channel(True).play(jump_sound)    #
Find a free channel or force use
            elif event.key == pygame.K_s:
                pygame.mixer.find_channel(True).play(shoot_sound)   #
Find a free channel or force use

    # Update the display
    pygame.display.flip()

# Quit PyGame
pygame.quit()
```

In this example, the `pygame.mixer.find_channel(True)` method finds a free channel or forces use of an existing one, optimizing channel management.

By implementing these optimization techniques, you can ensure smooth and responsive audio playback in your games, enhancing the overall player experience. Reducing latency, preloading sounds, using efficient audio formats, and managing sound channels effectively are key steps to optimizing audio performance in PyGame.

Chapter 7: Game Physics and Collision Detection

Basic Physics Principles in Games

Game physics are essential for creating a realistic and engaging gameplay experience. Physics principles dictate how objects move, interact, and react within the game environment. The key principles of game physics include motion, force, and collision. Understanding these principles allows developers to simulate real-world behaviors and enhance the player's immersion.

Motion is the foundation of game physics. It involves the movement of objects over time and can be described using parameters such as position, velocity, and acceleration. Position defines the location of an object in the game world, velocity is the rate of change of position, and acceleration is the rate of change of velocity. These parameters can be controlled and manipulated using physics equations.

Force is another critical aspect of game physics. It is the push or pull on an object that causes it to move or change its state of motion. Newton's laws of motion provide the basis for understanding how forces affect objects. The first law states that an object will remain at rest or in uniform motion unless acted upon by a force. The second law states that the force acting on an object is equal to the mass of the object times its acceleration (F = ma). The third law states that for every action, there is an equal and opposite reaction.

Collision detection and response are essential for creating realistic interactions between objects. Collision detection involves determining when two or more objects intersect or come into contact. There are various techniques for collision detection, including bounding boxes, circles, and more complex shapes like polygons. Once a collision is detected, the game must respond appropriately, often by applying forces, changing velocities, or triggering specific game events.

One of the simplest forms of motion is linear motion, which can be described using basic kinematic equations. For example, the position of an object moving at a constant velocity can be calculated as:

```
position = initial_position + velocity * time
```

For objects with acceleration, the position can be calculated using:

```
position = initial_position + initial_velocity * time + 0.5 * acceleration * time^2
```

Gravity is a common force in games, especially for platformers and physics-based puzzles. Gravity can be simulated by applying a constant acceleration downwards. In PyGame, you can simulate gravity by updating an object's velocity and position each frame:

```
gravity = 9.8
velocity_y += gravity * delta_time
position_y += velocity_y * delta_time
```

Friction is another important force, representing the resistance that one surface or object encounters when moving over another. It can be simulated by reducing an object's velocity over time:

```
friction = 0.1
velocity_x *= (1 - friction)
```

By combining these basic principles and equations, developers can create a wide range of physical behaviors in their games. Whether it's the simple falling of an object under gravity, the complex interactions of a physics-based puzzle game, or the realistic movement of characters and vehicles, understanding and applying physics principles is crucial for game development.

Implementing Gravity and Movement

Implementing gravity and movement in a game involves simulating the effects of gravity on objects and allowing them to move within the game world. Gravity is a force that pulls objects towards the ground, creating a sense of weight and realism. Movement, on the other hand, encompasses the ability of objects to navigate the game space, responding to player input and other forces.

To start, we need to define the gravitational acceleration, which is typically a constant value. In most 2D games, gravity acts in the downward direction. Here's a simple implementation of gravity in PyGame:

```
GRAVITY = 0.5

class GameObject:
    def __init__(self, x, y):
        self.x = x
        self.y = y
        self.velocity_y = 0
```

```python
def apply_gravity(self):
    self.velocity_y += GRAVITY
    self.y += self.velocity_y

def update(self):
    self.apply_gravity()
```

In this example, each `GameObject` has an initial position (x, y) and a vertical velocity `velocity_y`. The `apply_gravity` method increases the velocity by the gravity constant and updates the object's position accordingly.

Movement is typically controlled by player input. For instance, if we want an object to move left or right based on keyboard input, we can modify the object's position directly:

```python
def handle_input(self):
    keys = pygame.key.get_pressed()
    if keys[pygame.K_LEFT]:
        self.x -= 5
    if keys[pygame.K_RIGHT]:
        self.x += 5

def update(self):
    self.handle_input()
    self.apply_gravity()
```

Jumping is a common movement mechanic that involves temporarily overcoming gravity. To implement jumping, we apply an upward force when the player presses the jump key:

```python
JUMP_STRENGTH = -10

def handle_input(self):
    keys = pygame.key.get_pressed()
    if keys[pygame.K_LEFT]:
        self.x -= 5
    if keys[pygame.K_RIGHT]:
        self.x += 5
    if keys[pygame.K_SPACE] and self.on_ground():
        self.velocity_y = JUMP_STRENGTH

def on_ground(self):
```

```python
    # Placeholder for ground collision detection
    return self.y >= GROUND_LEVEL

def update(self):
    self.handle_input()
    self.apply_gravity()
```

In this example, `JUMP_STRENGTH` is a negative value to apply an upward force. The `on_ground` method checks if the object is on the ground, allowing it to jump only when it is not in the air.

Collision detection with the ground is crucial to prevent objects from falling indefinitely. A simple approach is to check the object's position and reset it when it goes below a certain level:

```python
GROUND_LEVEL = 500

def apply_gravity(self):
    self.velocity_y += GRAVITY
    self.y += self.velocity_y
    if self.y > GROUND_LEVEL:
        self.y = GROUND_LEVEL
        self.velocity_y = 0
```

By combining these elements—gravity, player-controlled movement, and collision detection with the ground—we can create a basic but functional movement system for our game characters.

Collision Detection Techniques

Collision detection is a fundamental aspect of game development, ensuring that objects interact realistically within the game world. Various techniques can be employed, depending on the complexity and requirements of the game. Here, we'll explore some common collision detection methods: bounding boxes, circles, and pixel-perfect detection.

Bounding Boxes

A bounding box is a simple rectangle that surrounds an object. Checking for collisions between bounding boxes is straightforward and efficient, making it suitable for many 2D games.

```python
def check_collision(rect1, rect2):
```

```
    return rect1.colliderect(rect2)

# Example usage
player_rect   =   pygame.Rect(player.x,    player.y,    player.width,
player.height)
enemy_rect   =   pygame.Rect(enemy.x,    enemy.y,    enemy.width,
enemy.height)

if check_collision(player_rect, enemy_rect):
    print("Collision detected!")
```

Circles

Circular collision detection is useful for objects that are better represented by circles, such as balls. The collision check involves calculating the distance between the centers of the circles and comparing it to the sum of their radii.

```
import math

def check_circle_collision(circle1, circle2):
    distance = math.sqrt((circle1.x - circle2.x) ** 2 + (circle1.y - circle2.y) ** 2)
    return distance < (circle1.radius + circle2.radius)

# Example usage
player_circle = Circle(player.x, player.y, player.radius)
enemy_circle = Circle(enemy.x, enemy.y, enemy.radius)

if check_circle_collision(player_circle, enemy_circle):
    print("Collision detected!")
```

Pixel-Perfect Detection

Pixel-perfect collision detection is more precise but computationally expensive. It checks for overlapping pixels between two objects, ensuring accurate collision results.

```
def check_pixel_collision(surface1, surface2, offset_x, offset_y):
    for x in range(surface1.get_width()):
        for y in range(surface1.get_height()):
            if surface1.get_at((x, y)).a != 0:
```

```
                if surface2.get_at((x + offset_x, y + offset_y)).a
!= 0:
                    return True
    return False

# Example usage
offset_x = enemy.x - player.x
offset_y = enemy.y - player.y

if check_pixel_collision(player_surface, enemy_surface, offset_x,
offset_y):
    print("Collision detected!")
```

Spatial Partitioning

For games with many objects, spatial partitioning techniques like grids or quadtrees can improve collision detection efficiency by reducing the number of checks required.

```
class Quadtree:
    def __init__(self, boundary, capacity):
        self.boundary = boundary
        self.capacity = capacity
        self.points = []
        self.divided = False

    def insert(self, point):
        if not self.boundary.contains(point):
            return False
        if len(self.points) < self.capacity:
            self.points.append(point)
            return True
        if not self.divided:
            self.subdivide()
        return (self.northeast.insert(point) or
                self.northwest.insert(point) or
                self.southeast.insert(point) or
                self.southwest.insert(point))

    def subdivide(self):
        # Code to subdivide the quadtree into four quadrants
        pass
```

113 | Chapter 7: Game Physics and Collision Detection

In this example, a quadtree is used to divide the game world into smaller regions, allowing for more efficient collision checks by only testing objects within the same region.

By selecting and combining these techniques, developers can create robust and efficient collision detection systems tailored to their game's needs.

Handling Collisions and Responses

Once collisions are detected, the next step is to handle them appropriately. This involves determining how objects should respond to collisions, which can include stopping movement, bouncing off surfaces, or triggering specific game events. Handling collisions effectively ensures a realistic and engaging gameplay experience.

Stopping Movement

One of the simplest responses to a collision is to stop the movement of the colliding objects. This is common in platformer games, where a character should stop falling when landing on the ground.

```
def handle_collision(player, ground):
    if player.rect.colliderect(ground.rect):
        player.velocity_y = 0
        player.y = ground.rect.top - player.height

# Example usage
handle_collision(player, ground)
```

Bouncing Off Surfaces

For more dynamic interactions, objects can bounce off surfaces. This requires reversing the velocity component perpendicular to the collision surface and possibly reducing it to simulate energy loss.

```
def handle_bounce(player, wall):
    if player.rect.colliderect(wall.rect):
        player.velocity_x = -player.velocity_x * 0.8    # Reduce velocity to simulate energy loss

# Example usage
handle_bounce(player, wall)
```

Sliding Along Surfaces

In some cases, objects should slide along surfaces rather than stopping or bouncing. This is common in top-down games where characters slide along walls.

```
def handle_slide(player, wall):
    if player.rect.colliderect(wall.rect):
        if abs(player.rect.right - wall.rect.left) < 10 or abs(player.rect.left - wall.rect.right) < 10:
            player.velocity_x = 0
        if abs(player.rect.bottom - wall.rect.top) < 10 or abs(player.rect.top - wall.rect.bottom) < 10:
            player.velocity_y = 0

# Example usage
handle_slide(player, wall)
```

Triggering Events

Collisions can also trigger specific game events, such as collecting an item, taking damage, or completing a level.

```
def handle_event(player, item):
    if player.rect.colliderect(item.rect):
        player.score += item.value
        item.collect()

# Example usage
handle_event(player, item)
```

Complex Collision Responses

For more complex interactions, such as character-enemy combat, a combination of responses may be required. This can include applying damage, playing animations, and updating game states.

```
def handle_combat(player, enemy):
    if player.rect.colliderect(enemy.rect):
        enemy.health -= player.attack_power
        if enemy.health <= 0:
            enemy.die()
```

```python
# Example usage
handle_combat(player, enemy)
```

Physics-Based Responses

In physics-based games, realistic collision responses can be achieved using physics engines. These engines handle the calculations for forces, impulses, and resulting movements, allowing for more accurate simulations.

```python
import pymunk

def handle_physics_collision(space):
    for collision in space.collisions:
        # Process the collision using physics engine
        pass

# Example usage
space.step(1/60.0)
handle_physics_collision(space)
```

By combining these collision handling techniques, developers can create diverse and engaging gameplay experiences. The key is to choose the appropriate response based on the type of game and the desired behavior of the objects involved.

Advanced Physics Simulations

Advanced physics simulations can add a layer of realism and complexity to a game, enhancing the overall player experience. These simulations often involve more detailed and accurate representations of physical phenomena, such as fluid dynamics, soft body dynamics, and ragdoll physics.

Fluid Dynamics

Simulating fluids can create realistic water, smoke, and other fluid-like behaviors. This involves solving the Navier-Stokes equations, which describe the motion of fluid substances.

```python
import numpy as np

# Simple fluid simulation using a grid-based approach
def simulate_fluid(grid, dt):
    for i in range(grid.shape[0]):
```

```python
        for j in range(grid.shape[1]):
            # Update velocity and pressure values based on fluid dynamics equations
            pass

# Example usage
grid = np.zeros((100, 100, 2))  # Grid with velocity vectors
simulate_fluid(grid, 1/60.0)
```

Soft Body Dynamics

Soft body dynamics simulate deformable objects, such as jelly or rubber. These simulations typically use a mass-spring model, where the object is represented by interconnected masses and springs.

```python
class SoftBody:
    def __init__(self, points, springs):
        self.points = points
        self.springs = springs

    def update(self, dt):
        for spring in self.springs:
            # Update positions of points based on spring forces
            pass

# Example usage
points = [(0, 0), (1, 0), (0, 1), (1, 1)]
springs = [(0, 1), (1, 3), (3, 2), (2, 0), (0, 3), (1, 2)]
soft_body = SoftBody(points, springs)
soft_body.update(1/60.0)
```

Ragdoll Physics

Ragdoll physics simulate the movement of a character's limbs in a realistic way when it falls or is impacted. This is often achieved using inverse kinematics and physics constraints.

```python
class Ragdoll:
    def __init__(self, joints, constraints):
        self.joints = joints
        self.constraints = constraints
```

```python
    def update(self, dt):
        for constraint in self.constraints:
            # Apply constraints to joints based on physics calculations
            pass

# Example usage
joints = [(0, 0), (0, 1), (1, 1), (1, 0)]
constraints = [(0, 1), (1, 2), (2, 3), (3, 0)]
ragdoll = Ragdoll(joints, constraints)
ragdoll.update(1/60.0)
```

Destruction Physics

Destruction physics simulate the breaking and shattering of objects. This can be achieved by dividing an object into smaller fragments and applying forces to each fragment.

```python
class DestructibleObject:
    def __init__(self, fragments):
        self.fragments = fragments

    def apply_force(self, force):
        for fragment in self.fragments:
            # Apply force to each fragment and update its position
            pass

# Example usage
fragments = [Fragment() for _ in range(10)]
destructible_object = DestructibleObject(fragments)
destructible_object.apply_force((10, 0))
```

Advanced Physics Engines

Using advanced physics engines like Box2D or Bullet can significantly simplify the implementation of complex simulations. These engines provide robust tools for handling various physical interactions and dynamics.

```python
import Box2D

# Example setup for a Box2D world
world = Box2D.b2World(gravity=(0, -10))
```

```
body = world.CreateDynamicBody(position=(0, 4))
box = body.CreatePolygonFixture(box=(1, 1), density=1, friction=0.3)

def update_world(world, dt):
    world.Step(dt, 6, 2)

# Example usage
update_world(world, 1/60.0)
```

By incorporating advanced physics simulations, developers can create more immersive and realistic game experiences. These simulations require a deeper understanding of physics principles and often involve more complex calculations and algorithms, but the results can be highly rewarding.

Chapter 8: Creating Game Levels

Designing Game Levels

Designing game levels is a crucial aspect of game development, as it directly impacts the player's experience and engagement. A well-designed level provides a balanced mix of challenges and rewards, guiding the player through the game while maintaining a sense of progression and discovery.

Understanding Level Design Principles

Level design involves creating the layout, pacing, and flow of a game level. Key principles include:

- **Balance:** Ensuring the level is neither too easy nor too difficult.
- **Flow:** Guiding the player smoothly through the level with clear objectives.
- **Variety:** Introducing new elements and challenges to keep the gameplay interesting.
- **Pacing:** Balancing moments of intense action with periods of rest or exploration.
- **Visuals:** Using visual cues to guide the player and create an immersive environment.

Sketching and Prototyping

Before diving into development, sketching the level layout on paper can help visualize the overall structure and flow. Prototyping the level in a simple form, using basic shapes and placeholders, allows for testing and refining the design without investing too much time in details.

Creating the Level Layout

The layout is the foundation of the level, defining the placement of platforms, obstacles, enemies, and other interactive elements. In a 2D platformer, this might involve arranging platforms and gaps to create jumping challenges, while in a top-down shooter, it could mean designing corridors and open areas for combat.

Adding Challenges and Obstacles

Challenges and obstacles are essential for keeping the player engaged. These can include enemies, traps, puzzles, and environmental hazards. The key is to introduce these elements progressively, increasing the difficulty as the player advances through the level.

Implementing Visual Design

Visual design enhances the level by creating an immersive and aesthetically pleasing environment. This involves choosing a theme, designing backgrounds and foregrounds, and placing decorative elements. Visual cues, such as lighting and color contrast, can also help guide the player.

Testing and Iterating

Testing the level is crucial for identifying issues and areas for improvement. Playtesting with a diverse group of players can provide valuable feedback. Iterating on the design based on this feedback ensures the level is polished and enjoyable.

Example: Creating a Basic Platformer Level in PyGame

```python
import pygame

# Initialize PyGame
pygame.init()

# Set up the display
screen = pygame.display.set_mode((800, 600))
pygame.display.set_caption("Platformer Level")

# Define colors
WHITE = (255, 255, 255)
BLACK = (0, 0, 0)

# Define the player
player = pygame.Rect(50, 500, 50, 50)

# Define platforms
platforms = [
    pygame.Rect(0, 550, 800, 50),
    pygame.Rect(200, 400, 100, 20),
    pygame.Rect(400, 300, 100, 20),
    pygame.Rect(600, 200, 100, 20)
]

# Main game loop
running = True
while running:
    for event in pygame.event.get():
        if event.type == pygame.QUIT:
            running = False

    # Handle player movement
    keys = pygame.key.get_pressed()
    if keys[pygame.K_LEFT]:
```

```
        player.x -= 5
    if keys[pygame.K_RIGHT]:
        player.x += 5
    if keys[pygame.K_SPACE]:
        player.y -= 10  # Simple jump

    # Gravity
    player.y += 5

    # Collision detection with platforms
    for platform in platforms:
        if player.colliderect(platform):
            player.y = platform.y - player.height

    # Draw everything
    screen.fill(WHITE)
    pygame.draw.rect(screen, BLACK, player)
    for platform in platforms:
        pygame.draw.rect(screen, BLACK, platform)

    pygame.display.flip()
    pygame.time.Clock().tick(60)

pygame.quit()
```

This example sets up a basic platformer level with a player and platforms. The player can move left and right and jump, with simple gravity and collision detection implemented. This basic setup can be expanded upon with more complex level designs, additional challenges, and refined visual elements.

Using Tile Maps

Tile maps are a powerful and flexible way to create game levels, especially for 2D games. They involve dividing the game world into a grid of tiles, each representing a small piece of the environment, such as ground, walls, or decorations. Tile maps simplify level design, allowing developers to create complex layouts efficiently.

Understanding Tile Maps

A tile map is essentially a 2D array where each element corresponds to a tile in the game world. Each tile has specific properties, such as its type, appearance, and behavior. Tile maps are often used in platformers, RPGs, and strategy games to create large, detailed environments.

Creating Tile Sets

A tile set is a collection of individual tiles that can be used to construct a tile map. Each tile is a small image, typically of uniform size, representing a piece of the environment. Tile sets are often stored in a single image file, with tiles arranged in a grid.

Loading and Rendering Tile Maps in PyGame

To use tile maps in PyGame, we need to load the tile set image, extract individual tiles, and render them based on the tile map data. Here's an example of how to achieve this:

```python
import pygame

# Initialize PyGame
pygame.init()

# Set up the display
screen = pygame.display.set_mode((800, 600))
pygame.display.set_caption("Tile Map Example")

# Load the tile set image
tile_set = pygame.image.load("tileset.png")

# Define the size of each tile
TILE_SIZE = 32

# Define a simple tile map (2D array)
tile_map = [
    [0, 0, 1, 1, 1, 0, 0],
    [0, 1, 1, 0, 1, 1, 0],
    [1, 1, 0, 0, 0, 1, 1],
    [0, 1, 1, 1, 1, 1, 0],
    [0, 0, 1, 1, 1, 0, 0]
]

# Function to draw the tile map
def draw_tile_map(screen, tile_map, tile_set, tile_size):
    for y, row in enumerate(tile_map):
        for x, tile in enumerate(row):
            tile_rect = pygame.Rect(tile * tile_size, 0, tile_size, tile_size)
            screen.blit(tile_set, (x * tile_size, y * tile_size), tile_rect)
```

```python
# Main game loop
running = True
while running:
    for event in pygame.event.get():
        if event.type == pygame.QUIT:
            running = False

    # Draw the tile map
    screen.fill((255, 255, 255))
    draw_tile_map(screen, tile_map, tile_set, TILE_SIZE)

    pygame.display.flip()
    pygame.time.Clock().tick(60)

pygame.quit()
```

In this example, the tile set image is loaded, and individual tiles are extracted and rendered based on the tile map data. The `draw_tile_map` function iterates over the tile map array and draws the corresponding tile at each position.

Editing Tile Maps

Tile maps can be created and edited using various tools, such as Tiled, a popular open-source map editor. Tiled allows developers to design tile maps visually, saving them in standard formats like JSON or TMX. These maps can then be loaded and used in PyGame.

Implementing Tile-Based Collision Detection

Collision detection in tile-based games involves checking the player's position against the tile map to determine if they are colliding with solid tiles. Here's an example of how to implement tile-based collision detection:

```python
def check_collision(player_rect, tile_map, tile_size):
    for y, row in enumerate(tile_map):
        for x, tile in enumerate(row):
            if tile == 1:  # Assuming 1 represents a solid tile
                tile_rect = pygame.Rect(x * tile_size, y * tile_size, tile_size, tile_size)
                if player_rect.colliderect(tile_rect):
                    return True
    return False
```

```
# Example usage
player_rect = pygame.Rect(50, 50, 32, 32)
if check_collision(player_rect, tile_map, TILE_SIZE):
    print("Collision detected!")
```

In this example, the `check_collision` function iterates over the tile map and checks if the player's rectangle intersects with any solid tile rectangles. This basic approach can be expanded to handle more complex collision responses and tile types.

By using tile maps, developers can create detailed and dynamic game levels efficiently. Tile maps offer flexibility in level design and simplify the process of creating and editing game environments.

Implementing Level Transitions

Level transitions are essential for providing a smooth and cohesive gameplay experience. They involve moving the player from one level to another, often with visual or gameplay effects to enhance immersion. Implementing level transitions requires careful planning and handling of game state changes.

Understanding Level Transitions

A level transition typically occurs when the player reaches a specific point in the level, completes certain objectives, or triggers an event. The transition can involve various effects, such as fading in and out, sliding screens, or cutscenes.

Triggering Level Transitions

Level transitions can be triggered by specific conditions, such as reaching an exit point or defeating a boss. These triggers can be implemented using collision detection or event handling.

```
def check_exit(player_rect, exit_rect):
    return player_rect.colliderect(exit_rect)

# Example usage
exit_rect = pygame.Rect(700, 500, 50, 50)
if check_exit(player_rect, exit_rect):
    print("Level complete! Transitioning to the next level.")
```

Loading and Unloading Levels

Chapter 8: Creating Game Levels

When transitioning between levels, it's important to load the new level's data and unload the current level's data to free up resources. This typically involves loading new tile maps, enemy placements, and other level-specific elements.

```
def load_level(level_data):
    # Load the level data, such as tile map, enemies, and objects
    pass

def unload_level():
    # Unload the current level's data
    pass

# Example usage
current_level = 1
if check_exit(player_rect, exit_rect):
    unload_level()
    current_level += 1
    load_level(level_data[current_level])
```

Creating Transition Effects

Transition effects enhance the visual experience during level changes. Common effects include fading in and out, sliding screens, and cutscenes.

Fade Effect

```
def fade_out(screen):
    fade_surface = pygame.Surface(screen.get_size())
    fade_surface.fill((0, 0, 0))
    for alpha in range(0, 256, 5):
        fade_surface.set_alpha(alpha)
        screen.blit(fade_surface, (0, 0))
        pygame.display.flip()
        pygame.time.delay(30)

def fade_in(screen):
    fade_surface = pygame.Surface(screen.get_size())
    fade_surface.fill((0, 0, 0))
    for alpha in range(255, -1, -5):
        fade_surface.set_alpha(alpha)
        screen.blit(fade_surface, (0, 0))
```

```
        pygame.display.flip()
        pygame.time.delay(30)

# Example usage
if check_exit(player_rect, exit_rect):
    fade_out(screen)
    unload_level()
    current_level += 1
    load_level(level_data[current_level])
    fade_in(screen)
```

Sliding Screen Effect

```
def slide_screen(screen, direction):
    width, height = screen.get_size()
    slide_surface = screen.copy()
    for offset in range(0, width, 20):
        if direction == "left":
            screen.blit(slide_surface, (-offset, 0))
        elif direction == "right":
            screen.blit(slide_surface, (offset, 0))
        pygame.display.flip()
        pygame.time.delay(30)

# Example usage
if check_exit(player_rect, exit_rect):
    slide_screen(screen, "right")
    unload_level()
    current_level += 1
    load_level(level_data[current_level])
    slide_screen(screen, "left")
```

Cutscenes

Cutscenes can provide narrative context and enhance the storytelling experience. They can be implemented using pre-rendered videos or scripted sequences within the game engine.

```
def play_cutscene(cutscene_file):
    # Play the cutscene video or scripted sequence
    pass
```

```python
# Example usage
if check_exit(player_rect, exit_rect):
    play_cutscene("cutscene.mp4")
    unload_level()
    current_level += 1
    load_level(level_data[current_level])
```

By implementing level transitions effectively, developers can create a seamless and engaging experience for players. These transitions provide a sense of progression and enhance the overall narrative and gameplay flow.

Creating and Managing Level Data

Creating and managing level data involves organizing and storing the information needed to construct and run each level in the game. This includes the layout, objects, enemies, and other elements that make up the level. Efficiently managing this data is crucial for scalability and ease of maintenance.

Defining Level Data Structures

Level data can be stored in various formats, such as JSON, XML, or custom binary formats. JSON is a popular choice due to its readability and ease of use.

Example JSON Level Data

```
{
    "tile_map": [
        [0, 0, 1, 1, 1, 0, 0],
        [0, 1, 1, 0, 1, 1, 0],
        [1, 1, 0, 0, 0, 1, 1],
        [0, 1, 1, 1, 1, 1, 0],
        [0, 0, 1, 1, 1, 0, 0]
    ],
    "player_start": {"x": 50, "y": 500},
    "enemies": [
        {"type": "goomba", "x": 200, "y": 400},
        {"type": "goomba", "x": 400, "y": 300}
    ],
    "exit": {"x": 700, "y": 500}
}
```

Loading Level Data

To load level data from a JSON file, we can use Python's built-in `json` module.

```python
import json

def load_level_data(file_path):
    with open(file_path, 'r') as file:
        level_data = json.load(file)
    return level_data

# Example usage
level_data = load_level_data('level1.json')
```

Creating Level Objects

Once the level data is loaded, we can create the game objects based on this data.

```python
def create_level(level_data):
    tile_map = level_data['tile_map']
    player_start = level_data['player_start']
    enemies = level_data['enemies']
    exit_position = level_data['exit']

    # Create player
    player = Player(player_start['x'], player_start['y'])

    # Create enemies
    enemy_objects = []
    for enemy_data in enemies:
        enemy   =   Enemy(enemy_data['type'],   enemy_data['x'], enemy_data['y'])
        enemy_objects.append(enemy)

    # Create exit
    exit_rect = pygame.Rect(exit_position['x'], exit_position['y'], 50, 50)

    return player, enemy_objects, exit_rect

# Example usage
```

```
player, enemies, exit_rect = create_level(level_data)
```

Managing Level Progression

Level progression involves moving the player from one level to the next and saving their progress. This can be achieved by keeping track of the current level and updating it upon completion.

```
current_level = 1

def load_next_level():
    global current_level
    current_level += 1
    level_data = load_level_data(f'level{current_level}.json')
    return create_level(level_data)

# Example usage
if check_exit(player_rect, exit_rect):
    player, enemies, exit_rect = load_next_level()
```

Saving and Loading Game Progress

To enhance the player experience, it's important to save and load game progress. This can be implemented by saving the current level and player state to a file.

Saving Progress

```
def save_progress(file_path, current_level, player_state):
    progress_data = {
        "current_level": current_level,
        "player_state": player_state
    }
    with open(file_path, 'w') as file:
        json.dump(progress_data, file)

# Example usage
player_state = {"x": player.x, "y": player.y, "health": player.health}
save_progress('savegame.json', current_level, player_state)
```

Loading Progress

```
def load_progress(file_path):
    with open(file_path, 'r') as file:
        progress_data = json.load(file)
    return progress_data

# Example usage
progress_data = load_progress('savegame.json')
current_level = progress_data['current_level']
player_state = progress_data['player_state']
level_data = load_level_data(f'level{current_level}.json')
player, enemies, exit_rect = create_level(level_data)
player.x = player_state['x']
player.y = player_state['y']
player.health = player_state['health']
```

By effectively creating and managing level data, developers can streamline the process of designing, implementing, and maintaining game levels. This approach also facilitates level progression and ensures a consistent and enjoyable player experience.

Level Testing and Optimization

Testing and optimizing game levels is essential to ensure a smooth, enjoyable, and bug-free player experience. This process involves identifying and fixing issues, improving performance, and balancing gameplay elements.

Playtesting

Playtesting is the process of having real players play the game to identify issues and gather feedback. It helps uncover problems that might not be apparent to the developers, such as unclear objectives, difficult sections, or unintended behaviors.

Organizing Playtesting Sessions

1. **Recruit Testers:** Find a diverse group of players, including both experienced and new players.
2. **Prepare Test Builds:** Create builds of your game that include specific levels or features you want to test.
3. **Collect Feedback:** Provide testers with a way to give feedback, such as surveys or interviews.

Analyzing Feedback

After collecting feedback, analyze it to identify common issues and areas for improvement. Prioritize the most critical issues and create a plan to address them.

Automated Testing

Automated testing involves creating scripts and tools to test various aspects of the game without human intervention. This can help identify issues more efficiently and ensure consistent testing coverage.

Example: Automated Collision Testing

```
def automated_collision_test(player, level_data):
    # Simulate player movement and check for collisions
    for step in range(1000):
        player.x += player.velocity_x
        player.y += player.velocity_y
        if   check_collision(player.rect,   level_data['tile_map'], TILE_SIZE):
            return False
    return True

# Example usage
if not automated_collision_test(player, level_data):
    print("Collision issue detected!")
```

Performance Optimization

Optimizing performance ensures the game runs smoothly on target hardware. This involves profiling the game to identify bottlenecks and implementing optimization techniques.

Profiling the Game

Profiling tools can help identify performance bottlenecks by measuring the time taken by various parts of the game code.

Example: Using cProfile

```
import cProfile

def game_loop():
    # Main game loop code
    pass
```

```
# Example usage
cProfile.run('game_loop()')
```

Optimizing Rendering

Rendering can be a significant performance bottleneck. Optimizing rendering involves reducing the number of draw calls, using efficient data structures, and leveraging hardware acceleration.

Batch Rendering

Batch rendering groups similar rendering commands together to reduce the number of draw calls.

```
def batch_render(sprites):
    for sprite in sprites:
        screen.blit(sprite.image, sprite.rect)

# Example usage
sprites = [sprite1, sprite2, sprite3]
batch_render(sprites)
```

Level of Detail (LOD)

Level of Detail (LOD) techniques involve rendering objects at different levels of detail based on their distance from the camera. This reduces the rendering workload for distant objects.

Example: Implementing LOD

```
def render_with_lod(camera, objects):
    for obj in objects:
        distance = calculate_distance(camera, obj)
        if distance < NEAR_DISTANCE:
            obj.render_high_detail(screen)
        elif distance < FAR_DISTANCE:
            obj.render_medium_detail(screen)
        else:
            obj.render_low_detail(screen)

# Example usage
render_with_lod(camera, objects)
```

Memory Management

Efficient memory management is crucial for preventing memory leaks and ensuring the game runs smoothly. This involves managing assets, optimizing data structures, and minimizing memory usage.

Example: Asset Management

```python
class AssetManager:
    def __init__(self):
        self.assets = {}

    def load_asset(self, name, file_path):
        if name not in self.assets:
            self.assets[name] = pygame.image.load(file_path)
        return self.assets[name]

# Example usage
asset_manager = AssetManager()
player_image = asset_manager.load_asset('player', 'player.png')
```

Balancing Gameplay

Balancing gameplay ensures the game is challenging but fair. This involves adjusting various parameters, such as enemy strength, player abilities, and resource availability.

Example: Balancing Enemy Health

```python
def balance_enemy_health(enemies, player_level):
    for enemy in enemies:
        enemy.health = base_health + (player_level * health_multiplier)

# Example usage
balance_enemy_health(enemies, player.level)
```

By thoroughly testing and optimizing game levels, developers can create a polished and enjoyable player experience. This process involves a combination of playtesting, automated testing, performance optimization, and gameplay balancing.

Level Testing and Optimization

Testing and optimizing game levels is essential to ensure a smooth, enjoyable, and bug-free player experience. This process involves identifying and fixing issues, improving performance, and balancing gameplay elements.

Playtesting

Playtesting is the process of having real players play the game to identify issues and gather feedback. It helps uncover problems that might not be apparent to the developers, such as unclear objectives, difficult sections, or unintended behaviors.

Organizing Playtesting Sessions

1. **Recruit Testers:** Find a diverse group of players, including both experienced and new players.
2. **Prepare Test Builds:** Create builds of your game that include specific levels or features you want to test.
3. **Collect Feedback:** Provide testers with a way to give feedback, such as surveys or interviews.

Analyzing Feedback

After collecting feedback, analyze it to identify common issues and areas for improvement. Prioritize the most critical issues and create a plan to address them.

Automated Testing

Automated testing involves creating scripts and tools to test various aspects of the game without human intervention. This can help identify issues more efficiently and ensure consistent testing coverage.

Example: Automated Collision Testing

```
def automated_collision_test(player, level_data):
    # Simulate player movement and check for collisions
    for step in range(1000):
        player.x += player.velocity_x
        player.y += player.velocity_y
        if  check_collision(player.rect,   level_data['tile_map'], TILE_SIZE):
            return False
    return True

# Example usage
if not automated_collision_test(player, level_data):
    print("Collision issue detected!")
```

Performance Optimization

Optimizing performance ensures the game runs smoothly on target hardware. This involves profiling the game to identify bottlenecks and implementing optimization techniques.

Profiling the Game

Profiling tools can help identify performance bottlenecks by measuring the time taken by various parts of the game code.

Example: Using cProfile

```python
import cProfile

def game_loop():
    # Main game loop code
    pass

# Example usage
cProfile.run('game_loop()')
```

Optimizing Rendering

Rendering can be a significant performance bottleneck. Optimizing rendering involves reducing the number of draw calls, using efficient data structures, and leveraging hardware acceleration.

Batch Rendering

Batch rendering groups similar rendering commands together to reduce the number of draw calls.

```python
def batch_render(sprites):
    for sprite in sprites:
        screen.blit(sprite.image, sprite.rect)

# Example usage
sprites = [sprite1, sprite2, sprite3]
batch_render(sprites)
```

Level of Detail (LOD)

Level of Detail (LOD) techniques involve rendering objects at different levels of detail based on their distance from the camera. This reduces the rendering workload for distant objects.

Example: Implementing LOD

```python
def render_with_lod(camera, objects):
    for obj in objects:
        distance = calculate_distance(camera, obj)
        if distance < NEAR_DISTANCE:
            obj.render_high_detail(screen)
        elif distance < FAR_DISTANCE:
            obj.render_medium_detail(screen)
        else:
            obj.render_low_detail(screen)

# Example usage
render_with_lod(camera, objects)
```

Memory Management

Efficient memory management is crucial for preventing memory leaks and ensuring the game runs smoothly. This involves managing assets, optimizing data structures, and minimizing memory usage.

Example: Asset Management

```python
class AssetManager:
    def __init__(self):
        self.assets = {}

    def load_asset(self, name, file_path):
        if name not in self.assets:
            self.assets[name] = pygame.image.load(file_path)
        return self.assets[name]

# Example usage
asset_manager = AssetManager()
player_image = asset_manager.load_asset('player', 'player.png')
```

Balancing Gameplay

Balancing gameplay ensures the game is challenging but fair. This involves adjusting various parameters, such as enemy strength, player abilities, and resource availability.

Example: Balancing Enemy Health

```
def balance_enemy_health(enemies, player_level):
    for enemy in enemies:
        enemy.health = base_health + (player_level * health_multiplier)

# Example usage
balance_enemy_health(enemies, player.level)
```

By thoroughly testing and optimizing game levels, developers can create a polished and enjoyable player experience. This process involves a combination of playtesting, automated testing, performance optimization, and gameplay balancing.

Chapter 9: Character Development and AI

Designing Player Characters

Designing player characters is a crucial aspect of game development. The player character is the avatar through which the player interacts with the game world, and it must be designed with care to ensure a compelling and engaging experience.

To begin with, the design process should focus on the character's visual appearance. This includes defining the character's physical attributes such as height, build, and distinguishing features. It is essential to create a character that is visually appealing and fits well within the game's aesthetic and story.

Next, the character's abilities and attributes need to be outlined. This includes deciding on the character's skills, strengths, and weaknesses. For example, a character in a platformer game might have the ability to jump high, run fast, or use specific tools. These abilities should align with the game's mechanics and contribute to the overall gameplay experience.

The character's personality is another critical element. This can be conveyed through dialogue, actions, and interactions with other characters. A well-developed personality makes the character relatable and memorable, enhancing the player's emotional connection to the game.

In terms of implementation, player character design involves creating character sprites or models. For 2D games, this means designing sprite sheets with various animations such as walking, jumping, and attacking. In PyGame, this can be achieved using the `pygame.sprite.Sprite` class to manage the different states and animations of the character.

```
class Player(pygame.sprite.Sprite):
    def __init__(self, x, y):
        super().__init__()
        self.image = pygame.image.load('player_idle.png')
        self.rect = self.image.get_rect()
        self.rect.topleft = (x, y)
        self.velocity = 5

    def update(self):
        keys = pygame.key.get_pressed()
        if keys[pygame.K_LEFT]:
            self.rect.x -= self.velocity
```

```
        if keys[pygame.K_RIGHT]:
            self.rect.x += self.velocity
        if keys[pygame.K_UP]:
            self.rect.y -= self.velocity
        if keys[pygame.K_DOWN]:
            self.rect.y += self.velocity
```

In this example, a basic player character is created with movement capabilities using the arrow keys.

Finally, the player character's interactions with the game environment must be designed. This includes collision detection with obstacles, enemies, and other interactive elements. Properly handling these interactions ensures smooth gameplay and prevents frustration for the player.

In summary, designing player characters involves a combination of visual design, defining abilities and personality, creating sprites or models, and implementing interactions within the game. Each of these components contributes to creating a character that enhances the player's engagement and enjoyment of the game.

Creating Non-Player Characters (NPCs)

Non-Player Characters (NPCs) play a vital role in enriching the game world and providing depth to the narrative. NPCs can serve various functions such as allies, enemies, merchants, or quest givers. Designing NPCs requires careful consideration of their roles, behaviors, and interactions with the player.

The first step in creating NPCs is defining their purpose within the game. This involves determining their role in the story and how they will interact with the player. For example, an NPC could provide valuable information, offer quests, or serve as a formidable opponent. Understanding the NPC's role helps shape their design and behavior.

Once the role is defined, the next step is to design the NPC's appearance. This includes creating character sprites or models that match the game's visual style. The design should reflect the NPC's personality and role. For instance, a wise old sage might have a long beard and robes, while a fierce warrior would have armor and weapons.

Behavior design is crucial for NPCs, especially those that interact dynamically with the player. This involves programming the NPC's actions, reactions, and dialogues. In PyGame, behavior can be implemented using state machines or scripting systems that define how NPCs respond to various events.

```
class NPC(pygame.sprite.Sprite):
    def __init__(self, x, y):
        super().__init__()
```

```
        self.image = pygame.image.load('npc.png')
        self.rect = self.image.get_rect()
        self.rect.topleft = (x, y)
        self.dialogue = ["Hello, traveler!", "Can you help me find
my lost sheep?"]

    def interact(self, player):
        if self.rect.colliderect(player.rect):
            for line in self.dialogue:
                print(line)
```

In this example, an NPC is created with a simple interaction that prints dialogue lines when the player is nearby.

The behavior design should also include how NPCs move and interact with the environment. This can involve pathfinding algorithms to navigate the game world or simple scripted movements. Ensuring NPCs behave believably and consistently enhances the game's immersion.

Finally, NPCs can have unique attributes and abilities that make them stand out. For example, an enemy NPC might have special attacks or defenses, while a merchant NPC could offer rare items. These attributes should be balanced to maintain game difficulty and player engagement.

In conclusion, creating NPCs involves defining their role, designing their appearance, implementing behavior and interactions, and giving them unique attributes. Well-designed NPCs contribute significantly to the depth and richness of the game world, making the player's experience more immersive and engaging.

Basic AI Concepts

Artificial Intelligence (AI) is essential for creating dynamic and responsive game environments. Basic AI concepts involve programming entities to exhibit behaviors that mimic human-like actions. These behaviors can range from simple movements to complex decision-making processes.

One of the fundamental AI concepts is state machines. A state machine consists of a set of states and transitions between those states based on specific conditions. For example, an enemy AI might have states such as Idle, Patrol, Chase, and Attack. The transitions between these states depend on conditions like the player's proximity or health level.

```
class Enemy(pygame.sprite.Sprite):
    def __init__(self, x, y):
        super().__init__()
```

```python
        self.image = pygame.image.load('enemy_idle.png')
        self.rect = self.image.get_rect()
        self.rect.topleft = (x, y)
        self.state = "Idle"

    def update(self, player):
        if self.state == "Idle":
            self.idle()
        elif self.state == "Patrol":
            self.patrol()
        elif self.state == "Chase" and self.detect_player(player):
            self.chase(player)
        elif self.state == "Attack" and self.in_attack_range(player):
            self.attack(player)

    def idle(self):
        pass

    def patrol(self):
        pass

    def chase(self, player):
        pass

    def attack(self, player):
        pass

    def detect_player(self, player):
        # Detection logic
        return True

    def in_attack_range(self, player):
        # Range check logic
        return True
```

This example demonstrates a simple state machine for an enemy AI, with states and transition conditions.

Pathfinding is another crucial AI concept, enabling NPCs to navigate the game world. The A* (A-star) algorithm is commonly used for pathfinding due to its efficiency and accuracy. A* finds the shortest path from a start point to a destination by considering the cost of each move and the estimated distance to the goal.

```python
def astar_pathfinding(start, goal, grid):
    open_set = set()
    open_set.add(start)
    came_from = {}
    g_score = {start: 0}
    f_score = {start: heuristic(start, goal)}

    while open_set:
        current = min(open_set, key=lambda x: f_score.get(x, float('inf')))
        if current == goal:
            return reconstruct_path(came_from, current)

        open_set.remove(current)
        for neighbor in get_neighbors(current, grid):
            tentative_g_score = g_score[current] + distance(current, neighbor)
            if tentative_g_score < g_score.get(neighbor, float('inf')):
                came_from[neighbor] = current
                g_score[neighbor] = tentative_g_score
                f_score[neighbor] = g_score[neighbor] + heuristic(neighbor, goal)
                open_set.add(neighbor)
    return []

def heuristic(a, b):
    return abs(a[0] - b[0]) + abs(a[1] - b[1])

def reconstruct_path(came_from, current):
    path = [current]
    while current in came_from:
        current = came_from[current]
        path.append(current)
    path.reverse()
    return path
```

This implementation of the A* algorithm finds the shortest path on a grid-based map.

Decision trees are another AI technique used for making choices based on a series of conditions. Each node in the tree represents a decision point, leading to different outcomes. Decision trees are useful for creating complex AI behaviors without hardcoding every possible scenario.

In summary, basic AI concepts such as state machines, pathfinding, and decision trees are fundamental for creating intelligent and responsive game entities. These techniques allow developers to design NPCs and other game elements that enhance the gameplay experience through realistic and dynamic behaviors.

Implementing Pathfinding

Pathfinding is a critical component in game AI, enabling characters to navigate complex environments efficiently. Implementing pathfinding involves using algorithms to determine the shortest or most efficient path between two points in the game world. One of the most popular pathfinding algorithms is A* (A-star), known for its balance of accuracy and efficiency.

To implement pathfinding, the game world needs to be represented in a way that the algorithm can process. This typically involves creating a grid or graph where each node represents a position in the game world. Obstacles and walkable areas are marked, allowing the algorithm to navigate around them.

```
class Grid:
    def __init__(self, width, height):
        self.width = width
        self.height = height
        self.nodes = [[Node(x, y) for y in range(height)] for x in range(width)]

class Node:
    def __init__(self, x, y, walkable=True):
        self.x = x
        self.y = y
        self.walkable = walkable
        self.g = 0
        self.h = 0
        self.f = 0
        self.parent = None
```

In this example, a `Grid` class is created to represent the game world, with each `Node` representing a position that can be either walkable or blocked by an obstacle.

The A* algorithm is then used to find the shortest path from a start node to a goal node. A* works by evaluating nodes based on their cost from the start node (g), their estimated cost to the goal node (h), and their total cost (f = g + h).

```python
def astar_pathfinding(grid, start, goal):
    open_set = set()
    closed_set = set()
    open_set.add(start)

    while open_set:
        current = min(open_set, key=lambda node: node.f)
        if current == goal:
            return reconstruct_path(current)

        open_set.remove(current)
        closed_set.add(current)

        for neighbor in get_neighbors(grid, current):
            if neighbor in closed_set or not neighbor.walkable:
                continue

            tentative_g = current.g + distance(current, neighbor)
            if neighbor not in open_set:
                open_set.add(neighbor)
            elif tentative_g >= neighbor.g:
                continue

            neighbor.parent = current
            neighbor.g = tentative_g
            neighbor.h = heuristic(neighbor, goal)
            neighbor.f = neighbor.g + neighbor.h

    return []

def get_neighbors(grid, node):
    neighbors = []
    for dx, dy in [(-1, 0), (1, 0), (0, -1), (0, 1)]:
        x, y = node.x + dx, node.y + dy
        if 0 <= x < grid.width and 0 <= y < grid.height:
            neighbors.append(grid.nodes[x][y])
    return neighbors
```

```python
def distance(node1, node2):
    return abs(node1.x - node2.x) + abs(node1.y - node2.y)

def heuristic(node, goal):
    return abs(node.x - goal.x) + abs(node.y - goal.y)

def reconstruct_path(node):
    path = []
    while node:
        path.append((node.x, node.y))
        node = node.parent
    path.reverse()
    return path
```

This code demonstrates a complete implementation of the A* algorithm. The `astar_pathfinding` function takes a grid, start node, and goal node as inputs, and returns the shortest path as a list of coordinates.

Pathfinding can be further optimized by using techniques such as hierarchical pathfinding, where the game world is divided into regions, and paths are first found between regions before finding detailed paths within regions. Additionally, smoothing algorithms can be applied to paths to make them more natural and less grid-like.

In conclusion, implementing pathfinding is essential for creating intelligent and efficient AI in games. Using algorithms like A* and optimizing them for specific game requirements ensures that characters can navigate the game world effectively, providing a better gameplay experience for players.

Advanced AI Behaviors

Advanced AI behaviors add depth and complexity to game characters, making them more realistic and challenging. These behaviors go beyond basic state machines and pathfinding, incorporating techniques such as behavior trees, neural networks, and machine learning.

Behavior trees are a powerful tool for implementing complex AI behaviors. They are hierarchical structures that organize actions and conditions in a tree format, allowing for flexible and modular AI design. Each node in the tree represents an action or a decision point, and the tree can be dynamically adjusted based on the game state.

```python
class BehaviorTree:
    def __init__(self, root):
        self.root = root
```

```python
    def tick(self):
        self.root.tick()

class Selector:
    def __init__(self, children):
        self.children = children

    def tick(self):
        for child in self.children:
            if child.tick():
                return True
        return False

class Sequence:
    def __init__(self, children):
        self.children = children

    def tick(self):
        for child in self.children:
            if not child.tick():
                return False
        return True

class Action:
    def __init__(self, action):
        self.action = action

    def tick(self):
        return self.action()
```

In this example, a simple behavior tree framework is implemented with selectors, sequences, and actions.

Neural networks and machine learning techniques can also be used to create adaptive and intelligent AI. These methods involve training AI models using data to recognize patterns and make decisions. For instance, a neural network can be trained to predict player movements and adapt its strategy accordingly.

```python
from keras.models import Sequential
from keras.layers import Dense
```

```python
import numpy as np

# Create a neural network model
model = Sequential()
model.add(Dense(64, input_dim=4, activation='relu'))
model.add(Dense(32, activation='relu'))
model.add(Dense(1, activation='sigmoid'))

# Compile the model
model.compile(loss='binary_crossentropy',          optimizer='adam',
metrics=['accuracy'])

# Generate training data
data = np.random.rand(1000, 4)
labels = np.random.randint(2, size=(1000, 1))

# Train the model
model.fit(data, labels, epochs=10, batch_size=10)

# Use the model for predictions
predictions = model.predict(np.random.rand(10, 4))
```

This code demonstrates a basic neural network using Keras for training and predictions.

Advanced AI behaviors also involve learning and adapting to player actions. Reinforcement learning, for example, enables AI to learn optimal behaviors through trial and error, receiving rewards for positive actions and penalties for negative ones. This approach allows AI to improve over time and adapt to different playstyles.

```python
import numpy as np

class QLearningAgent:
    def __init__(self, state_size, action_size):
        self.state_size = state_size
        self.action_size = action_size
        self.q_table = np.zeros((state_size, action_size))
        self.alpha = 0.1   # Learning rate
        self.gamma = 0.9   # Discount factor
        self.epsilon = 0.1   # Exploration rate

    def choose_action(self, state):
```

```python
        if np.random.rand() < self.epsilon:
            return np.random.randint(self.action_size)
        return np.argmax(self.q_table[state])

    def update_q_table(self, state, action, reward, next_state):
        best_next_action = np.argmax(self.q_table[next_state])
        td_target = reward + self.gamma * self.q_table[next_state][best_next_action]
        self.q_table[state][action] += self.alpha * (td_target - self.q_table[state][action])
```

This code snippet demonstrates a basic Q-learning agent for reinforcement learning.

In summary, advanced AI behaviors enhance the complexity and realism of game characters. Techniques such as behavior trees, neural networks, and reinforcement learning allow developers to create adaptive, intelligent, and challenging AI that significantly improves the gameplay experience.

Chapter 10: Game State Management

Understanding Game States

Game state management is crucial for maintaining and transitioning between different states within a game. A game state represents a specific condition or mode in the game, such as the main menu, gameplay, pause screen, or game over screen. Properly managing these states ensures a smooth and coherent gameplay experience.

To start, it's essential to understand the various states that a game can have. Common game states include:

- **Main Menu:** The initial screen where players can start the game, adjust settings, or view credits.
- **Gameplay:** The primary state where the core game mechanics and player interactions occur.
- **Pause:** A state that temporarily halts gameplay, allowing players to take a break or access in-game menus.
- **Game Over:** The state displayed when the player loses or completes the game.
- **Loading:** A transitional state used to load resources or switch between levels.

Each state requires specific handling and transitions. Implementing a state management system involves creating a structure that can switch between these states seamlessly. One common approach is using a finite state machine (FSM).

```python
class GameState:
    def __init__(self):
        self.states = {}
        self.current_state = None

    def add_state(self, name, state):
        self.states[name] = state

    def set_state(self, name):
        self.current_state = self.states[name]

    def update(self):
        if self.current_state:
            self.current_state.update()

    def render(self, screen):
        if self.current_state:
```

```
            self.current_state.render(screen)

class MenuState:
    def update(self):
        pass  # Handle menu logic

    def render(self, screen):
        pass  # Render menu

class PlayState:
    def update(self):
        pass  # Handle gameplay logic

    def render(self, screen):
        pass  # Render gameplay
```

In this example, a simple FSM is implemented with `GameState` managing different states like `MenuState` and `PlayState`.

Transitions between states should be handled smoothly. For instance, transitioning from the main menu to gameplay might involve fading effects or loading screens. Proper transition management ensures that the game does not abruptly switch states, which can be jarring for players.

Another critical aspect of game state management is preserving the game context. When transitioning between states, relevant data such as player progress, score, and settings should be retained. This can be achieved by using global variables or passing context objects between states.

```
class GameContext:
    def __init__(self):
        self.score = 0
        self.level = 1

context = GameContext()

class PlayState:
    def __init__(self, context):
        self.context = context

    def update(self):
        self.context.score += 1  # Update score
```

```python
def render(self, screen):
    pass  # Render gameplay
```

In this example, `GameContext` holds the game state data, and `PlayState` updates and uses this data.

In summary, understanding game states and implementing a robust state management system is essential for creating a cohesive and enjoyable gaming experience. By clearly defining states, managing transitions, and preserving context, developers can ensure that players have a smooth and engaging journey through the game.

Implementing Menus and HUDs

Menus and Heads-Up Displays (HUDs) are integral components of a game's user interface. They provide players with essential information and allow them to interact with the game through options and settings. Implementing these elements effectively enhances the overall user experience.

To begin with, menus serve as the primary navigation points in a game. They include the main menu, settings menu, pause menu, and other in-game menus. Designing menus involves creating visually appealing layouts that are intuitive and easy to navigate. Each menu should have buttons or options that respond to user inputs.

In PyGame, creating a menu can be achieved by rendering text and handling input events. Here's an example of a basic main menu:

```python
class MainMenu:
    def __init__(self):
        self.font = pygame.font.Font(None, 74)
        self.options = ["Start Game", "Settings", "Quit"]
        self.selected_option = 0

    def update(self):
        keys = pygame.key.get_pressed()
        if keys[pygame.K_UP]:
            self.selected_option = (self.selected_option - 1) % len(self.options)
        if keys[pygame.K_DOWN]:
            self.selected_option = (self.selected_option + 1) % len(self.options)
        if keys[pygame.K_RETURN]:
            self.select_option()
```

```python
    def render(self, screen):
        screen.fill((0, 0, 0))
        for i, option in enumerate(self.options):
            color = (255, 0, 0) if i == self.selected_option else (255, 255, 255)
            text = self.font.render(option, True, color)
            screen.blit(text, (100, 100 + i * 100))

    def select_option(self):
        if self.selected_option == 0:
            # Start Game
            pass
        elif self.selected_option == 1:
            # Settings
            pass
        elif self.selected_option == 2:
            pygame.quit()
            exit()
```

In this example, `MainMenu` handles the rendering and navigation of menu options. The selected option changes based on the arrow keys, and pressing Enter triggers the selected option.

HUDs, on the other hand, provide in-game information such as health, score, and ammo count. HUD elements should be non-intrusive but easily visible to the player. They are typically rendered on top of the game screen and updated continuously during gameplay.

Here's an example of a simple HUD displaying the player's health and score:

```python
class HUD:
    def __init__(self, player):
        self.player = player
        self.font = pygame.font.Font(None, 36)

    def render(self, screen):
        health_text = self.font.render(f"Health: {self.player.health}", True, (255, 255, 255))
        score_text = self.font.render(f"Score: {self.player.score}", True, (255, 255, 255))
        screen.blit(health_text, (10, 10))
        screen.blit(score_text, (10, 50))
```

In this example, the `HUD` class takes a `player` object and renders the player's health and score on the screen.

It's important to design menus and HUDs to be responsive and adaptable to different screen sizes and resolutions. This ensures that the user interface looks good and functions well on various devices. Using layout managers and scaling techniques can help achieve this adaptability.

In conclusion, implementing menus and HUDs involves designing intuitive layouts, handling user inputs, and ensuring responsiveness. These elements play a crucial role in providing a smooth and enjoyable user experience, guiding players through the game and keeping them informed during gameplay.

Saving and Loading Game Progress

Saving and loading game progress is a vital feature in modern games, allowing players to continue their adventures from where they left off. Implementing this feature involves creating mechanisms to store and retrieve game state data, ensuring that all relevant information is preserved accurately.

To begin with, it's essential to determine what data needs to be saved. This typically includes the player's position, health, inventory, score, level, and any other state-specific information. Organizing this data into a structured format makes it easier to save and load.

One common approach is to use JSON (JavaScript Object Notation) for storing game data due to its simplicity and readability. Here's an example of how to save and load game progress using JSON in Python:

```python
import json

class GameData:
    def __init__(self, player):
        self.player = player

    def save(self, filename):
        data = {
            'position': (self.player.rect.x, self.player.rect.y),
            'health': self.player.health,
            'score': self.player.score,
            'level': self.player.level
        }
        with open(filename, 'w') as file:
            json.dump(data, file)
```

```
    def load(self, filename):
        with open(filename, 'r') as file:
            data = json.load(file)
            self.player.rect.x,         self.player.rect.y           =
data['position']
            self.player.health = data['health']
            self.player.score = data['score']
            self.player.level = data['level']
```

In this example, `GameData` handles saving and loading the player's state to and from a JSON file. The `save` method converts the player's state into a dictionary and writes it to a file, while the `load` method reads the file and updates the player's state accordingly.

To integrate saving and loading into the game, you can add options in the main menu or pause menu to trigger these actions. Here's an example of how to add a save and load option to a menu:

```
class MainMenu:
    def __init__(self, game_data):
        self.font = pygame.font.Font(None, 74)
        self.options = ["Start Game", "Save Game", "Load Game", "Quit"]
        self.selected_option = 0
        self.game_data = game_data

    def update(self):
        keys = pygame.key.get_pressed()
        if keys[pygame.K_UP]:
            self.selected_option = (self.selected_option - 1) % len(self.options)
        if keys[pygame.K_DOWN]:
            self.selected_option = (self.selected_option + 1) % len(self.options)
        if keys[pygame.K_RETURN]:
            self.select_option()

    def render(self, screen):
        screen.fill((0, 0, 0))
        for i, option in enumerate(self.options):
```

```python
                color = (255, 0, 0) if i == self.selected_option else
(255, 255, 255)
                text = self.font.render(option, True, color)
                screen.blit(text, (100, 100 + i * 100))

    def select_option(self):
        if self.selected_option == 0:
            # Start Game
            pass
        elif self.selected_option == 1:
            self.game_data.save('savegame.json')
        elif self.selected_option == 2:
            self.game_data.load('savegame.json')
        elif self.selected_option == 3:
            pygame.quit()
            exit()
```

In this example, `MainMenu` includes options to save and load the game, interacting with the `GameData` instance.

Ensuring data integrity and handling errors are crucial when implementing save and load features. It's important to check if the save file exists and handle scenarios where loading might fail due to file corruption or other issues.

```python
def load(self, filename):
    try:
        with open(filename, 'r') as file:
            data = json.load(file)
            self.player.rect.x,        self.player.rect.y        =
data['position']
            self.player.health = data['health']
            self.player.score = data['score']
            self.player.level = data['level']
    except (FileNotFoundError, json.JSONDecodeError):
        print("Failed to load game data. Starting a new game.")
```

In this enhanced `load` method, errors are caught, and a message is displayed if loading fails.

In summary, saving and loading game progress involves determining the necessary data to store, using structured formats like JSON, and integrating these features into the game's user interface. Proper error handling and data integrity checks ensure a reliable and user-friendly experience for players.

Managing Game Loops

The game loop is the core of any game, responsible for updating the game state, processing user inputs, and rendering the graphics. Managing the game loop efficiently is crucial for maintaining smooth and responsive gameplay. A well-structured game loop ensures that all aspects of the game are handled in a timely and organized manner.

A typical game loop consists of three main phases: processing input, updating the game state, and rendering the graphics. These phases are repeated continuously, usually within a fixed time frame or frame rate.

Here's an example of a basic game loop in PyGame:

```
import pygame

pygame.init()
screen = pygame.display.set_mode((800, 600))
clock = pygame.time.Clock()

running = True
while running:
    # Process input
    for event in pygame.event.get():
        if event.type == pygame.QUIT:
            running = False

    # Update game state
    # (Update logic here)

    # Render graphics
    screen.fill((0, 0, 0))
    # (Rendering logic here)
    pygame.display.flip()

    # Cap the frame rate
    clock.tick(60)

pygame.quit()
```

Chapter 10: Game State Management

In this example, the game loop processes input events, updates the game state, renders the graphics, and caps the frame rate to 60 frames per second.

Processing input involves handling events such as keyboard and mouse inputs. This phase ensures that player actions are captured and responded to in real-time. The event loop processes all pending events, allowing the game to react accordingly.

Updating the game state is where the core game logic resides. This includes moving characters, checking for collisions, updating scores, and other game mechanics. It's important to keep the update logic efficient to maintain a high frame rate and responsive gameplay.

Rendering the graphics involves drawing the game world, characters, UI elements, and any other visual components. The screen is typically cleared at the beginning of each frame, and then all elements are drawn in the correct order.

Managing the game loop also involves handling timing and synchronization. Using a fixed time step ensures that the game runs consistently on different hardware, regardless of the frame rate. This can be achieved by calculating the time elapsed since the last frame and using it to update the game state.

```python
import time

previous_time = time.time()
while running:
    current_time = time.time()
    delta_time = current_time - previous_time
    previous_time = current_time

    # Process input
    for event in pygame.event.get():
        if event.type == pygame.QUIT:
            running = False

    # Update game state
    # (Update logic here, using delta_time for consistency)

    # Render graphics
    screen.fill((0, 0, 0))
    # (Rendering logic here)
    pygame.display.flip()

    # Cap the frame rate
    clock.tick(60)
```

In this example, `delta_time` is used to ensure consistent updates regardless of the frame rate.

Another aspect of managing game loops is handling different game states, such as menus, gameplay, and pause screens. Using a finite state machine (FSM) can help organize and manage these states within the game loop.

```python
class Game:
    def __init__(self):
        self.state = "menu"

    def update(self, delta_time):
        if self.state == "menu":
            self.update_menu()
        elif self.state == "play":
            self.update_play(delta_time)
        elif self.state == "pause":
            self.update_pause()

    def update_menu(self):
        pass  # Handle menu logic

    def update_play(self, delta_time):
        pass  # Handle gameplay logic

    def update_pause(self):
        pass  # Handle pause logic

game = Game()
while running:
    current_time = time.time()
    delta_time = current_time - previous_time
    previous_time = current_time

    # Process input
    for event in pygame.event.get():
        if event.type == pygame.QUIT:
            running = False

    # Update game state
```

```python
        game.update(delta_time)

        # Render graphics
        screen.fill((0, 0, 0))
        # (Rendering logic here)
        pygame.display.flip()

        # Cap the frame rate
        clock.tick(60)
```

In this example, the `Game` class manages different states and updates them accordingly within the game loop.

In summary, managing game loops effectively involves processing input, updating the game state, rendering graphics, handling timing, and organizing game states. A well-structured game loop ensures smooth and responsive gameplay, providing a better experience for players.

State Transition Management

State transition management is crucial for creating a seamless and immersive gameplay experience. Transitions occur when the game moves from one state to another, such as from the main menu to gameplay, or from gameplay to a pause screen. Managing these transitions smoothly ensures that players are not jarred by abrupt changes and can maintain their immersion in the game.

The first step in state transition management is defining the states and the conditions under which transitions occur. Common states include menus, gameplay, pause screens, and game over screens. Each state should have clear entry and exit points, with defined transitions based on player actions or game events.

To manage transitions, it's helpful to use a state machine framework. This framework tracks the current state and handles transitions based on predefined rules. Here's an example of a basic state machine for managing game states:

```python
class GameState:
    def __init__(self):
        self.states = {}
        self.current_state = None

    def add_state(self, name, state):
        self.states[name] = state
```

```python
    def set_state(self, name):
        self.current_state = self.states[name]

    def update(self):
        if self.current_state:
            self.current_state.update()

    def render(self, screen):
        if self.current_state:
            self.current_state.render(screen)

class MenuState:
    def update(self):
        pass  # Handle menu logic

    def render(self, screen):
        pass  # Render menu

class PlayState:
    def update(self):
        pass  # Handle gameplay logic

    def render(self, screen):
        pass  # Render gameplay
```

In this example, the `GameState` class manages different states like `MenuState` and `PlayState`, allowing for smooth transitions between them.

Transitions should be handled gracefully, often with visual or audio cues to signal the change to the player. This can include fading effects, transitions screens, or sound effects. Implementing these transitions enhances the player's experience and keeps the game feeling polished.

Here's an example of adding a fade transition between states:

```python
class FadeTransition:
    def __init__(self, duration):
        self.duration = duration
        self.alpha = 0
        self.direction = 1
```

```python
    def update(self, delta_time):
        self.alpha += self.direction * (255 / self.duration) * delta_time
        if self.alpha >= 255:
            self.alpha = 255
            self.direction = -1
        elif self.alpha <= 0:
            self.alpha = 0
            self.direction = 1

    def render(self, screen):
        fade_surface = pygame.Surface(screen.get_size())
        fade_surface.fill((0, 0, 0))
        fade_surface.set_alpha(self.alpha)
        screen.blit(fade_surface, (0, 0))
```

In this example, FadeTransition handles the fading effect, updating the alpha value and rendering a black surface with varying transparency.

To integrate state transitions with a fade effect, you can modify the state machine to include transition handling:

```python
class GameState:
    def __init__(self):
        self.states = {}
        self.current_state = None
        self.transition = None

    def add_state(self, name, state):
        self.states[name] = state

    def set_state(self, name, transition=None):
        self.current_state = self.states[name]
        self.transition = transition

    def update(self, delta_time):
        if self.transition:
            self.transition.update(delta_time)
            if self.transition.alpha == 0:
                self.transition = None
        else:
```

```
            if self.current_state:
                self.current_state.update(delta_time)

    def render(self, screen):
        if self.current_state:
            self.current_state.render(screen)
        if self.transition:
            self.transition.render(screen)
```

In this modified `GameState` class, a `transition` object is managed alongside the current state, ensuring that transitions are handled smoothly.

In summary, state transition management involves defining states, handling transitions gracefully, and using visual or audio cues to enhance the player's experience. Implementing a state machine framework and integrating transition effects ensures that state changes are smooth and immersive, contributing to a polished and enjoyable game.

Chapter 11: Multiplayer Game Development

Introduction to Multiplayer Games

Multiplayer games involve multiple players interacting with each other within the same game environment. These interactions can take place over a local network or the internet. Multiplayer games can range from cooperative gameplay, where players work together to achieve a common goal, to competitive gameplay, where players compete against each other. Understanding the fundamental concepts and architecture of multiplayer games is crucial for creating engaging and seamless multiplayer experiences.

Types of Multiplayer Games

Multiplayer games can be broadly categorized into several types, including:

- **Local Multiplayer:** Players use the same device or local network to interact.
- **Online Multiplayer:** Players connect over the internet, either in real-time or asynchronously.
- **Massively Multiplayer Online Games (MMOs):** A large number of players interact in a persistent game world.

Key Components of Multiplayer Games

Several key components are essential for developing multiplayer games:

- **Networking:** Establishing and maintaining connections between players.
- **Synchronization:** Ensuring all players see the same game state.
- **Latency Management:** Handling delays in data transmission.
- **Security:** Preventing cheating and protecting player data.

Challenges in Multiplayer Game Development

Developing multiplayer games presents unique challenges:

- **Network Latency:** Managing the delay in communication between players.
- **Data Consistency:** Ensuring all players have a consistent view of the game state.
- **Scalability:** Supporting a large number of concurrent players.
- **Security:** Protecting against hacking and cheating.

Choosing a Networking Model

There are two primary networking models for multiplayer games:

- **Peer-to-Peer (P2P):** Players connect directly to each other. This model is suitable for small-scale games but can be challenging to manage for larger games.
- **Client-Server:** A central server manages the game state and client connections. This model is more scalable and secure but requires more resources.

Tools and Frameworks

Various tools and frameworks can aid in developing multiplayer games:

- **Socket Libraries:** Libraries like Python's `socket` module for low-level network communication.
- **Game Development Frameworks:** Frameworks like Unity and Unreal Engine provide built-in networking capabilities.
- **Dedicated Servers:** Platforms like AWS and Google Cloud offer infrastructure for hosting game servers.

Example: Basic Networked Game

Here's a simple example of a networked game using Python's `socket` library:

```python
import socket

def start_server():
    server = socket.socket(socket.AF_INET, socket.SOCK_STREAM)
    server.bind(('localhost', 5555))
    server.listen(2)
    print("Server started, waiting for connections...")
    conn, addr = server.accept()
    print(f"Connected to {addr}")
    while True:
        data = conn.recv(1024)
        if not data:
            break
        print(f"Received: {data.decode()}")
        conn.sendall(data)
    conn.close()

def start_client():
    client = socket.socket(socket.AF_INET, socket.SOCK_STREAM)
    client.connect(('localhost', 5555))
    client.sendall(b"Hello, Server!")
    data = client.recv(1024)
    print(f"Received: {data.decode()}")
```

```
    client.close()

# Uncomment to run server or client
# start_server()
# start_client()
```

This basic example demonstrates setting up a simple server and client that can communicate over a local network.

Network Programming Basics

Network programming involves writing software that enables data exchange between computers over a network. This section covers the basics of network programming, essential for developing multiplayer games.

Understanding Networking Protocols

Networking protocols define rules for data exchange. The most common protocols used in multiplayer game development are:

- **TCP (Transmission Control Protocol):** Ensures reliable, ordered delivery of data.
- **UDP (User Datagram Protocol):** Offers faster, connectionless communication, but without guaranteed delivery.

Sockets and Connections

Sockets are endpoints for communication between two machines. In Python, the `socket` library provides the tools needed to create and manage sockets.

Creating a Basic Server

A server listens for incoming connections and processes client requests. Here's a basic example of a TCP server:

```
import socket

def start_server():
    server_socket = socket.socket(socket.AF_INET, socket.SOCK_STREAM)
    server_socket.bind(('localhost', 12345))
    server_socket.listen(5)
    print("Server listening on port 12345")
```

```
    while True:
        client_socket, addr = server_socket.accept()
        print(f"Connection from {addr}")
        client_socket.sendall(b"Hello, Client!")
        client_socket.close()

start_server()
```

Creating a Basic Client

A client connects to a server to send and receive data. Here's a basic example of a TCP client:

```
import socket

def start_client():
    client_socket            =            socket.socket(socket.AF_INET, socket.SOCK_STREAM)
    client_socket.connect(('localhost', 12345))
    data = client_socket.recv(1024)
    print(f"Received from server: {data.decode()}")
    client_socket.close()

start_client()
```

Handling Multiple Clients

To handle multiple clients, you can use threading or asynchronous programming. Here's an example using threading:

```
import socket
import threading

def handle_client(client_socket):
    request = client_socket.recv(1024)
    print(f"Received: {request.decode()}")
    client_socket.sendall(b"ACK")
    client_socket.close()

def start_server():
```

Chapter 11: Multiplayer Game Development

```
    server_socket = socket.socket(socket.AF_INET, socket.SOCK_STREAM)
    server_socket.bind(('localhost', 12345))
    server_socket.listen(5)
    print("Server listening on port 12345")

    while True:
        client_socket, addr = server_socket.accept()
        print(f"Connection from {addr}")
        client_handler = threading.Thread(target=handle_client, args=(client_socket,))
        client_handler.start()

start_server()
```

Using Asynchronous Programming

Asynchronous programming can handle many clients efficiently without creating a thread for each connection. Python's `asyncio` library is useful for this purpose.

Example: Asynchronous Server

Here's an example of an asynchronous server using `asyncio`:

```
import asyncio

async def handle_client(reader, writer):
    data = await reader.read(100)
    message = data.decode()
    print(f"Received: {message}")
    writer.write(data)
    await writer.drain()
    writer.close()

async def start_server():
    server = await asyncio.start_server(handle_client, 'localhost', 12345)
    async with server:
        await server.serve_forever()

asyncio.run(start_server())
```

Example: Asynchronous Client

Here's an example of an asynchronous client using `asyncio`:

```
import asyncio

async def start_client():
    reader, writer = await asyncio.open_connection('localhost', 12345)
    message = "Hello, Server!"
    writer.write(message.encode())
    data = await reader.read(100)
    print(f"Received: {data.decode()}")
    writer.close()

asyncio.run(start_client())
```

Conclusion

Understanding network programming basics is crucial for developing multiplayer games. By mastering sockets, threading, and asynchronous programming, you can create robust and scalable multiplayer game experiences.

Setting Up a Server-Client Architecture

Setting up a server-client architecture is fundamental for multiplayer game development. This architecture allows multiple clients (players) to connect to a central server, which manages the game state and synchronizes the clients.

Server-Client Model Overview

In a server-client model:

- **Server:** Manages the game state, handles client connections, and synchronizes data.
- **Client:** Connects to the server, sends user inputs, and receives updates.

Designing the Server

A well-designed server handles multiple clients efficiently, processes game logic, and maintains a consistent game state. Key considerations include:

- **Concurrency:** Using threading or asynchronous programming to handle multiple clients.
- **Data Integrity:** Ensuring the game state is consistent across all clients.
- **Security:** Preventing unauthorized access and cheating.

Implementing the Server

Here's an example of a simple server using Python's `socket` and `threading` libraries:

```python
import socket
import threading

clients = []

def handle_client(client_socket):
    while True:
        try:
            message = client_socket.recv(1024)
            if not message:
                break
            broadcast(message, client_socket)
        except:
            clients.remove(client_socket)
            client_socket.close()
            break

def broadcast(message, client_socket):
    for client in clients:
        if client != client_socket:
            client.send(message)

def start_server():
    server_socket = socket.socket(socket.AF_INET, socket.SOCK_STREAM)
    server_socket.bind(('localhost', 12345))
    server_socket.listen(5)
    print("Server listening on port 12345")

    while True:
        client_socket, addr = server_socket.accept()
        clients.append(client_socket)
        print(f"Connection from {addr}")
```

```
        client_handler   =   threading.Thread(target=handle_client,
args=(client_socket,))
        client_handler.start()

start_server()
```

Designing the Client

The client connects to the server, sends user inputs, and receives game state updates. Key considerations include:

- **Latency:** Minimizing delay in communication with the server.
- **Synchronization:** Ensuring the client's view of the game state is consistent with the server.
- **User Experience:** Providing a responsive and smooth gameplay experience.

Implementing the Client

Here's an example of a simple client using Python's `socket` library:

```
import socket

def start_client():
    client_socket                 =              socket.socket(socket.AF_INET, socket.SOCK_STREAM)
    client_socket.connect(('localhost', 12345))

    def receive_messages():
        while True:
            try:
                message = client_socket.recv(1024)
                print(f"Received: {message.decode()}")
            except:
                client_socket.close()
                break

    receive_thread = threading.Thread(target=receive_messages)
    receive_thread.start()

    while True:
        message = input("Enter message: ")
        client_socket.send(message.encode())
```

```
start_client()
```

Handling Game State Synchronization

Synchronizing the game state between the server and clients is critical. Common techniques include:

- **State Replication:** Regularly sending the entire game state to clients.
- **Delta Updates:** Sending only changes (deltas) to the game state.
- **Client-Side Prediction:** Predicting and updating the game state on the client side to reduce perceived latency.

Implementing State Synchronization

Here's an example of state synchronization using delta updates:

```
import json

game_state = {'players': {}}

def handle_client(client_socket):
    while True:
        try:
            message = client_socket.recv(1024)
            if not message:
                break
            update_state(message, client_socket)
        except:
            clients.remove(client_socket)
            client_socket.close()
            break

def update_state(message, client_socket):
    data = json.loads(message.decode())
    game_state['players'][client_socket] = data
    broadcast_state()

def broadcast_state():
    for client in clients:
        client.send(json.dumps(game_state).encode())
```

```
# Server setup code remains the same
```

Conclusion

Setting up a server-client architecture is essential for multiplayer game development. By designing efficient and secure server and client components, and implementing robust state synchronization, you can create engaging and scalable multiplayer games.

Handling Real-Time Multiplayer

Real-time multiplayer games require efficient handling of continuous player interactions and data synchronization. This section covers techniques and best practices for developing real-time multiplayer games.

Real-Time Multiplayer Challenges

Developing real-time multiplayer games presents several challenges:

- **Latency:** Minimizing the delay between player actions and their effects in the game.
- **Consistency:** Ensuring all players have a consistent view of the game state.
- **Bandwidth:** Managing the amount of data transmitted between clients and the server.

Techniques for Reducing Latency

Reducing latency is critical for real-time multiplayer games. Common techniques include:

- **Client-Side Prediction:** Predicting player movements and actions on the client side to reduce perceived latency.
- **Dead Reckoning:** Estimating the future position of moving objects based on their current velocity and direction.
- **Lag Compensation:** Adjusting the game state to account for network delays.

Implementing Client-Side Prediction

Client-side prediction involves predicting the outcome of player actions locally and then synchronizing with the server. Here's an example:

```
import time

player_position = [0, 0]

def predict_movement(direction, speed, delta_time):
    if direction == "UP":
```

```
        player_position[1] -= speed * delta_time
    elif direction == "DOWN":
        player_position[1] += speed * delta_time
    elif direction == "LEFT":
        player_position[0] -= speed * delta_time
    elif direction == "RIGHT":
        player_position[0] += speed * delta_time

def update_position_from_server(server_position):
    player_position[0] = server_position[0]
    player_position[1] = server_position[1]

# Example usage
start_time = time.time()
predict_movement("UP", 5, time.time() - start_time)
```

Dead Reckoning Technique

Dead reckoning involves estimating an object's future position based on its current state. This technique helps reduce the amount of data transmitted between clients and the server.

```
class Player:
    def __init__(self, position, velocity):
        self.position = position
        self.velocity = velocity

def dead_reckon(player, delta_time):
    player.position[0] += player.velocity[0] * delta_time
    player.position[1] += player.velocity[1] * delta_time

# Example usage
player = Player([0, 0], [1, 0])
dead_reckon(player, 0.1)
```

Lag Compensation

Lag compensation adjusts the game state to account for network delays, ensuring a fair experience for all players.

```
def compensate_lag(client_time, server_time, position, velocity):
```

```
    delta_time = server_time - client_time
    position[0] += velocity[0] * delta_time
    position[1] += velocity[1] * delta_time
    return position

# Example usage
compensated_position = compensate_lag(1.0, 1.2, [0, 0], [1, 0])
```

Synchronizing Game State

Synchronizing the game state involves regularly updating the clients with the latest game state from the server. Techniques include:

- **State Replication:** Regularly sending the entire game state to clients.
- **Delta Updates:** Sending only the changes (deltas) to the game state.

Example: Delta Updates

Here's an example of using delta updates for state synchronization:

```
import json

game_state = {'players': {}}

def handle_client(client_socket):
    while True:
        try:
            message = client_socket.recv(1024)
            if not message:
                break
            update_state(message, client_socket)
        except:
            clients.remove(client_socket)
            client_socket.close()
            break

def update_state(message, client_socket):
    data = json.loads(message.decode())
    game_state['players'][client_socket] = data
    broadcast_delta(data)

def broadcast_delta(delta):
```

```
        for client in clients:
            client.send(json.dumps(delta).encode())

# Server setup code remains the same
```

Implementing Real-Time Multiplayer with WebSockets

WebSockets provide a full-duplex communication channel over a single TCP connection, suitable for real-time multiplayer games.

Example: WebSocket Server with `websockets`

Here's an example of a WebSocket server using the `websockets` library:

```
import asyncio
import websockets

clients = set()

async def handle_client(websocket, path):
    clients.add(websocket)
    try:
        async for message in websocket:
            await broadcast(message)
    finally:
        clients.remove(websocket)

async def broadcast(message):
    for client in clients:
        if client.open:
            await client.send(message)

start_server = websockets.serve(handle_client, 'localhost', 12345)
asyncio.get_event_loop().run_until_complete(start_server)
asyncio.get_event_loop().run_forever()
```

Example: WebSocket Client

Here's an example of a WebSocket client using the `websockets` library:

```python
import asyncio
import websockets

async def start_client():
    async with websockets.connect('ws://localhost:12345') as websocket:
        await websocket.send("Hello, Server!")
        while True:
            message = await websocket.recv()
            print(f"Received: {message}")

asyncio.get_event_loop().run_until_complete(start_client())
```

Conclusion

Handling real-time multiplayer involves reducing latency, ensuring consistency, and managing bandwidth. Techniques like client-side prediction, dead reckoning, and lag compensation, combined with efficient state synchronization, are essential for developing responsive and engaging real-time multiplayer games.

Synchronizing Game States

Synchronizing game states across multiple clients is crucial for ensuring a consistent and fair gameplay experience in multiplayer games. This section covers various techniques and best practices for achieving effective game state synchronization.

Importance of Game State Synchronization

Game state synchronization ensures that all players see the same game world and events, despite network latency and other challenges. Proper synchronization prevents desynchronization, where different players have different views of the game state, leading to a poor user experience.

Techniques for Synchronizing Game States

Several techniques can be used to synchronize game states:

- **State Replication:** Sending the entire game state to clients at regular intervals.
- **Delta Updates:** Sending only the changes (deltas) to the game state.
- **Event-Based Updates:** Sending events that trigger state changes on the client side.

State Replication

State replication involves periodically sending the entire game state to all clients. This technique is simple to implement but can be bandwidth-intensive for large game states.

Example: State Replication

Here's an example of state replication in a simple multiplayer game:

```python
import json
import socket

game_state = {'players': {}}

def handle_client(client_socket):
    while True:
        try:
            message = client_socket.recv(1024)
            if not message:
                break
            update_state(message, client_socket)
        except:
            clients.remove(client_socket)
            client_socket.close()
            break

def update_state(message, client_socket):
    data = json.loads(message.decode())
    game_state['players'][client_socket] = data
    broadcast_state()

def broadcast_state():
    for client in clients:
        client.send(json.dumps(game_state).encode())

# Server setup code remains the same
```

Delta Updates

Delta updates involve sending only the changes (deltas) to the game state. This technique is more efficient than state replication but requires more complex state management.

Example: Delta Updates

Here's an example of using delta updates for state synchronization:

```python
import json

game_state = {'players': {}}

def handle_client(client_socket):
    while True:
        try:
            message = client_socket.recv(1024)
            if not message:
                break
            update_state(message, client_socket)
        except:
            clients.remove(client_socket)
            client_socket.close()
            break

def update_state(message, client_socket):
    data = json.loads(message.decode())
    game_state['players'][client_socket] = data
    broadcast_delta(data)

def broadcast_delta(delta):
    for client in clients:
        client.send(json.dumps(delta).encode())

# Server setup code remains the same
```

Event-Based Updates

Event-based updates involve sending events that trigger state changes on the client side. This technique reduces the amount of data transmitted but requires more complex client-side logic.

Example: Event-Based Updates

Here's an example of using event-based updates:

```python
import json

def handle_client(client_socket):
    while True:
```

```
        try:
            message = client_socket.recv(1024)
            if not message:
                break
            broadcast_event(message)
        except:
            clients.remove(client_socket)
            client_socket.close()
            break

def broadcast_event(event):
    for client in clients:
        client.send(event)

# Client-side event handling
def handle_event(event):
    data = json.loads(event)
    if data['type'] == 'MOVE':
        player_position = data['position']

# Server setup code remains the same
```

Handling Network Latency

Network latency can cause delays in state synchronization, leading to inconsistent game states. Techniques to handle latency include:

- **Client-Side Prediction:** Predicting state changes on the client side to reduce perceived latency.
- **Lag Compensation:** Adjusting the game state to account for network delays.

Example: Client-Side Prediction

Here's an example of client-side prediction for player movement:

```
import time

player_position = [0, 0]

def predict_movement(direction, speed, delta_time):
    if direction == "UP":
        player_position[1] -= speed * delta_time
```

```python
    elif direction == "DOWN":
        player_position[1] += speed * delta_time
    elif direction == "LEFT":
        player_position[0] -= speed * delta_time
    elif direction == "RIGHT":
        player_position[0] += speed * delta_time

def update_position_from_server(server_position):
    player_position[0] = server_position[0]
    player_position[1] = server_position[1]

# Example usage
start_time = time.time()
predict_movement("UP", 5, time.time() - start_time)
```

Conclusion

Synchronizing game states is essential for maintaining a consistent and fair multiplayer experience. By using techniques like state replication, delta updates, and event-based updates, and handling network latency through client-side prediction and lag compensation, you can achieve effective game state synchronization in your multiplayer games.

Chapter 12: Enhancing Game Performance

Profiling and Optimization Techniques

Enhancing game performance involves identifying performance bottlenecks and optimizing the code to run efficiently. Profiling tools and optimization techniques help developers improve game performance, leading to a smoother and more enjoyable player experience.

Importance of Profiling

Profiling is the process of measuring the performance of a program, identifying slow or resource-intensive parts of the code. Profiling helps developers understand where optimizations are needed and the impact of those optimizations.

Profiling Tools

Several profiling tools are available for Python and game development:

- **cProfile:** A built-in Python module for profiling.
- **line_profiler:** A tool for line-by-line profiling.
- **Py-Spy:** A sampling profiler for Python programs.
- **Pygame Performance Tools:** Built-in tools for profiling Pygame applications.

Using cProfile

cProfile is a built-in Python module that profiles the entire program. Here's an example of using cProfile to profile a Pygame application:

```python
import cProfile
import pygame

def main():
    pygame.init()
    screen = pygame.display.set_mode((800, 600))
    running = True
    while running:
        for event in pygame.event.get():
            if event.type == pygame.QUIT:
                running = False
        screen.fill((0, 0, 0))
        pygame.display.flip()
```

```
        pygame.quit()

if __name__ == "__main__":
    cProfile.run('main()')
```

Line-by-Line Profiling with line_profiler

line_profiler provides more granular profiling, allowing developers to see the time spent on each line of code. Here's an example:

```
from line_profiler import LineProfiler
import pygame

def main():
    pygame.init()
    screen = pygame.display.set_mode((800, 600))
    running = True
    while running:
        for event in pygame.event.get():
            if event.type == pygame.QUIT:
                running = False
        screen.fill((0, 0, 0))
        pygame.display.flip()
    pygame.quit()

if __name__ == "__main__":
    profiler = LineProfiler()
    profiler.add_function(main)
    profiler.run('main()')
    profiler.print_stats()
```

Identifying Bottlenecks

Profiling helps identify performance bottlenecks, such as:

- **CPU-bound Operations:** Intensive computations that slow down the game.
- **Memory Usage:** Excessive memory allocation leading to slowdowns.
- **Rendering Performance:** Inefficient rendering causing frame drops.

Optimizing Code

Once bottlenecks are identified, various optimization techniques can be applied:

- **Code Refactoring:** Simplifying complex code and removing redundant operations.
- **Efficient Data Structures:** Using appropriate data structures for better performance.
- **Caching:** Storing frequently accessed data in memory to reduce computation.
- **Asynchronous Programming:** Using asynchronous techniques to handle I/O-bound operations.

Example: Code Refactoring

Refactoring code for better performance can involve simplifying loops and reducing unnecessary computations:

```
# Before optimization
def update_positions(objects):
    for obj in objects:
        obj.x += obj.vx
        obj.y += obj.vy
        obj.vx *= 0.99
        obj.vy *= 0.99


# After optimization
def update_positions(objects):
    for obj in objects:
        obj.x += obj.vx
        obj.y += obj.vy
        obj.vx *= 0.99
        obj.vy *= 0.99
```

Efficient Data Structures

Choosing the right data structure can significantly improve performance. For example, using a dictionary for fast lookups instead of a list:

```
# Using a list
objects = [obj1, obj2, obj3]
for obj in objects:
    if obj.id == target_id:
        process(obj)

# Using a dictionary
objects = {obj1.id: obj1, obj2.id: obj2, obj3.id: obj3}
if target_id in objects:
```

```
    process(objects[target_id])
```

Caching Techniques

Caching can reduce the need for repetitive computations. Here's an example of using a simple cache:

```
cache = {}

def expensive_computation(x):
    if x in cache:
        return cache[x]
    result = x * x  # Simulate an expensive computation
    cache[x] = result
    return result
```

Asynchronous Programming

Asynchronous programming can improve performance by allowing the game to handle other tasks while waiting for I/O operations to complete. Here's an example using `asyncio`:

```
import asyncio

async def fetch_data():
    await asyncio.sleep(1)  # Simulate an I/O operation
    return "data"

async def main():
    data = await fetch_data()
    print(data)

asyncio.run(main())
```

Conclusion

Profiling and optimization are essential for enhancing game performance. By using profiling tools to identify bottlenecks and applying optimization techniques, developers can create smooth and efficient games that provide a better player experience.

Memory Management

Efficient memory management is crucial for enhancing game performance and ensuring the game runs smoothly without crashes or slowdowns. This section covers techniques for managing memory usage in game development.

Understanding Memory Usage

Memory usage refers to the amount of memory a game consumes while running. High memory usage can lead to performance issues, including slowdowns and crashes, especially on devices with limited memory.

Identifying Memory Leaks

Memory leaks occur when a program allocates memory but fails to release it, leading to increased memory usage over time. Identifying and fixing memory leaks is crucial for maintaining optimal performance.

Tools for Monitoring Memory Usage

Several tools are available for monitoring memory usage in Python:

- **gc Module:** Python's built-in garbage collector module.
- **objgraph:** A module for tracking and visualizing object references.
- **memory_profiler:** A module for monitoring memory usage line by line.

Using the gc Module

The `gc` module provides functions to interact with Python's garbage collector, which automatically manages memory allocation and deallocation. Here's an example of using the `gc` module to monitor memory usage:

```python
import gc
import time

def create_objects():
    for _ in range(100000):
        obj = object()

def monitor_memory():
    gc.collect()
    print(f"Garbage collector: {gc.get_count()}")
    time.sleep(1)

if __name__ == "__main__":
```

```
while True:
    create_objects()
    monitor_memory()
```

Using objgraph

`objgraph` helps visualize object references and identify memory leaks. Here's an example of using `objgraph` to track object creation:

```
import objgraph

def create_objects():
    objects = [object() for _ in range(100000)]
    return objects

if __name__ == "__main__":
    create_objects()
    objgraph.show_growth()
```

Using memory_profiler

`memory_profiler` provides line-by-line memory usage tracking. Here's an example:

```
from memory_profiler import profile

@profile
def create_objects():
    objects = [object() for _ in range(100000)]
    return objects

if __name__ == "__main__":
    create_objects()
```

Managing Memory Allocation

Efficient memory allocation involves minimizing unnecessary memory usage and releasing unused memory promptly. Techniques include:

- **Object Pooling:** Reusing objects instead of creating new ones.
- **Lazy Initialization:** Initializing objects only when needed.

- **Reference Counting:** Tracking the number of references to an object and deallocating it when no longer needed.

Example: Object Pooling

Object pooling involves reusing objects instead of creating and destroying them repeatedly. Here's an example:

```python
class ObjectPool:
    def __init__(self, create_func, size):
        self.pool = [create_func() for _ in range(size)]
        self.create_func = create_func

    def get(self):
        if self.pool:
            return self.pool.pop()
        return self.create_func()

    def release(self, obj):
        self.pool.append(obj)

def create_object():
    return object()

pool = ObjectPool(create_object, 10)
obj = pool.get()
pool.release(obj)
```

Example: Lazy Initialization

Lazy initialization involves creating objects only when they are needed. Here's an example:

```python
class LazyObject:
    def __init__(self):
        self._value = None

    @property
    def value(self):
        if self._value is None:
            self._value = self._initialize()
        return self._value
```

```python
    def _initialize(self):
        return "Expensive Initialization"

obj = LazyObject()
print(obj.value)
```

Conclusion

Efficient memory management is essential for maintaining game performance and preventing slowdowns or crashes. By using tools to monitor memory usage, identifying and fixing memory leaks, and applying memory optimization techniques, developers can create games that run smoothly and efficiently.

Reducing Lag and Latency

Reducing lag and latency is crucial for providing a smooth and responsive gameplay experience, especially in multiplayer games. This section covers techniques for minimizing lag and latency in game development.

Understanding Lag and Latency

- **Lag:** A delay between a player's action and the game's response.
- **Latency:** The time it takes for data to travel from the player to the server and back.

Causes of Lag and Latency

Several factors can cause lag and latency, including:

- **Network Delays:** Slow or unstable internet connections.
- **Server Load:** High server load leading to processing delays.
- **Client-Side Performance:** Poor performance on the player's device.

Techniques for Reducing Lag

Several techniques can help reduce lag in games:

- **Optimizing Network Code:** Efficient network code reduces data transmission delays.
- **Load Balancing:** Distributing the server load to prevent overload.
- **Client-Side Optimization:** Ensuring the game runs efficiently on the player's device.

Optimizing Network Code

Efficient network code reduces the amount of data transmitted and minimizes delays. Techniques include:

- **Data Compression:** Compressing data before transmission to reduce size.
- **Predictive Algorithms:** Predicting player actions to minimize perceived lag.
- **Efficient Protocols:** Using efficient networking protocols like UDP for real-time communication.

Example: Data Compression

Here's an example of using the `zlib` module for data compression:

```python
import zlib

data = b"Hello, World!" * 100
compressed_data = zlib.compress(data)
print(f"Original size: {len(data)}, Compressed size: {len(compressed_data)}")

decompressed_data = zlib.decompress(compressed_data)
print(decompressed_data == data)
```

Example: Predictive Algorithms

Predictive algorithms estimate future player actions to reduce perceived lag. Here's an example of a simple predictive algorithm:

```python
class Player:
    def __init__(self, position, velocity):
        self.position = position
        self.velocity = velocity

def predict_position(player, delta_time):
    predicted_position = [
        player.position[0] + player.velocity[0] * delta_time,
        player.position[1] + player.velocity[1] * delta_time
    ]
    return predicted_position

player = Player([0, 0], [1, 0])
predicted_position = predict_position(player, 0.1)
print(predicted_position)
```

Load Balancing

Load balancing involves distributing the server load to prevent overload. Techniques include:

- **Horizontal Scaling:** Adding more servers to distribute the load.
- **Geographic Distribution:** Placing servers in different locations to reduce latency for distant players.

Example: Horizontal Scaling

Horizontal scaling can be achieved using cloud services like AWS or Google Cloud. Here's a basic example of setting up multiple server instances:

```python
# Example using AWS SDK for Python (boto3)
import boto3

ec2 = boto3.resource('ec2')

def launch_instance():
    instance = ec2.create_instances(
        ImageId='ami-12345678',
        MinCount=1,
        MaxCount=1,
        InstanceType='t2.micro'
    )
    print(f"Launched instance: {instance[0].id}")

launch_instance()
```

Client-Side Optimization

Optimizing the game to run efficiently on the player's device can significantly reduce lag. Techniques include:

- **Efficient Rendering:** Reducing the complexity of rendering operations.
- **Resource Management:** Efficiently managing memory and CPU usage.
- **Frame Rate Optimization:** Ensuring a consistent frame rate.

Example: Efficient Rendering

Efficient rendering reduces the load on the GPU and CPU. Here's an example of optimizing rendering in Pygame:

```python
import pygame

def draw_objects(screen, objects):
    for obj in objects:
        pygame.draw.circle(screen, (255, 0, 0), obj['position'], obj['radius'])

pygame.init()
screen = pygame.display.set_mode((800, 600))
objects = [{'position': (400, 300), 'radius': 20} for _ in range(1000)]
running = True

while running:
    for event in pygame.event.get():
        if event.type == pygame.QUIT:
            running = False

    screen.fill((0, 0, 0))
    draw_objects(screen, objects)
    pygame.display.flip()

pygame.quit()
```

Conclusion

Reducing lag and latency is essential for providing a smooth and responsive gameplay experience. By optimizing network code, implementing load balancing, and ensuring client-side optimization, developers can minimize delays and improve the overall gaming experience.

Efficient Rendering Strategies

Efficient rendering is crucial for achieving high performance and smooth visuals in games. This section covers strategies and techniques for optimizing rendering in game development.

Understanding Rendering

Rendering is the process of generating images from a game's data, typically involving drawing objects, textures, and effects on the screen. Efficient rendering ensures that this process is fast and minimizes the load on the GPU and CPU.

Techniques for Efficient Rendering

Several techniques can help achieve efficient rendering:

- **Batch Rendering:** Grouping multiple draw calls into a single call to reduce overhead.
- **Level of Detail (LOD):** Adjusting the detail of objects based on their distance from the camera.
- **Frustum Culling:** Rendering only objects within the camera's view.
- **Occlusion Culling:** Rendering only objects that are not hidden behind others.

Batch Rendering

Batch rendering reduces the number of draw calls by grouping multiple objects into a single call. This technique minimizes the overhead associated with each draw call.

Example: Batch Rendering in Pygame

Here's an example of batch rendering in Pygame:

```
import pygame

def batch_draw(screen, objects, texture):
    for obj in objects:
        screen.blit(texture, obj['position'])

pygame.init()
screen = pygame.display.set_mode((800, 600))
texture = pygame.Surface((50, 50))
texture.fill((255, 0, 0))
objects = [{'position': (i * 60, 300)} for i in range(10)]
running = True

while running:
    for event in pygame.event.get():
        if event.type == pygame.QUIT:
            running = False

    screen.fill((0, 0, 0))
    batch_draw(screen, objects, texture)
    pygame.display.flip()

pygame.quit()
```

Level of Detail (LOD)

Level of Detail (LOD) adjusts the complexity of objects based on their distance from the camera, reducing the rendering load for distant objects.

Example: Level of Detail

Here's an example of implementing LOD:

```python
class Object:
    def __init__(self, position, high_detail, low_detail):
        self.position = position
        self.high_detail = high_detail
        self.low_detail = low_detail

    def draw(self, screen, camera_position):
        distance = abs(self.position[0] - camera_position[0])
        if distance < 100:
            screen.blit(self.high_detail, self.position)
        else:
            screen.blit(self.low_detail, self.position)

pygame.init()
screen = pygame.display.set_mode((800, 600))
high_detail = pygame.Surface((50, 50))
high_detail.fill((255, 0, 0))
low_detail = pygame.Surface((25, 25))
low_detail.fill((0, 255, 0))
objects = [Object((i * 60, 300), high_detail, low_detail) for i in range(10)]
running = True
camera_position = (0, 0)

while running:
    for event in pygame.event.get():
        if event.type == pygame.QUIT:
            running = False

    screen.fill((0, 0, 0))
    for obj in objects:
        obj.draw(screen, camera_position)
    pygame.display.flip()
```

```
pygame.quit()
```

Frustum Culling

Frustum culling involves rendering only objects within the camera's view, reducing the number of objects that need to be drawn.

Example: Frustum Culling

Here's an example of implementing frustum culling:

```
def is_in_frustum(position, frustum):
    x, y = position
    left, right, top, bottom = frustum
    return left <= x <= right and top <= y <= bottom

pygame.init()
screen = pygame.display.set_mode((800, 600))
objects = [{'position': (i * 60, 300)} for i in range(20)]
frustum = (0, 800, 0, 600)
running = True

while running:
    for event in pygame.event.get():
        if event.type == pygame.QUIT:
            running = False

    screen.fill((0, 0, 0))
    for obj in objects:
        if is_in_frustum(obj['position'], frustum):
            pygame.draw.circle(screen, (255, 0, 0), obj['position'], 20)
    pygame.display.flip()

pygame.quit()
```

Occlusion Culling

Occlusion culling involves rendering only objects that are not hidden behind others, reducing the rendering load.

Chapter 12: Enhancing Game Performance

Example: Occlusion Culling

Here's an example of implementing occlusion culling:

```python
def is_occluded(position, occluders):
    x, y = position
    for occluder in occluders:
        if occluder.collidepoint(x, y):
            return True
    return False

pygame.init()
screen = pygame.display.set_mode((800, 600))
objects = [{'position': (i * 60, 300)} for i in range(10)]
occluders = [pygame.Rect(200, 200, 200, 200)]
running = True

while running:
    for event in pygame.event.get():
        if event.type == pygame.QUIT:
            running = False

    screen.fill((0, 0, 0))
    for obj in objects:
        if not is_occluded(obj['position'], occluders):
            pygame.draw.circle(screen, (255, 0, 0), obj['position'], 20)
    for occluder in occluders:
        pygame.draw.rect(screen, (0, 255, 0), occluder)
    pygame.display.flip()

pygame.quit()
```

Conclusion

Efficient rendering strategies are essential for achieving high performance and smooth visuals in games. By using techniques like batch rendering, level of detail, frustum culling, and occlusion culling, developers can optimize rendering and enhance the overall gaming experience.

Optimizing for Different Platforms

Optimizing games for different platforms ensures that they run smoothly and efficiently across various devices and operating systems. This section covers techniques for platform-specific optimization in game development.

Understanding Platform Differences

Different platforms have varying hardware capabilities, operating systems, and performance characteristics. Optimizing for these differences is crucial for providing a consistent gaming experience.

Common Platforms

Common platforms for game development include:

- **PC (Windows, macOS, Linux):** Desktop platforms with varying hardware configurations.
- **Consoles (PlayStation, Xbox, Nintendo):** Gaming consoles with fixed hardware specifications.
- **Mobile (iOS, Android):** Mobile devices with limited resources and different operating systems.
- **Web:** Browser-based games with varying performance across browsers.

Techniques for Platform Optimization

Several techniques can help optimize games for different platforms:

- **Conditional Compilation:** Using platform-specific code and libraries.
- **Resource Management:** Managing memory and assets efficiently based on platform capabilities.
- **Input Handling:** Adapting input methods to the target platform.
- **Performance Profiling:** Profiling and optimizing performance for each platform.

Conditional Compilation

Conditional compilation involves using platform-specific code and libraries to optimize performance. Here's an example in Python:

```python
import platform

if platform.system() == "Windows":
    # Windows-specific code
    import ctypes
    ctypes.windll.user32.MessageBoxW(0, "Hello, Windows!", "Platform", 1)
elif platform.system() == "Darwin":
    # macOS-specific code
```

```
    import subprocess
    subprocess.call(['osascript', '-e', 'display notification
"Hello, macOS!" with title "Platform"'])
else:
    # Linux-specific code
    print("Hello, Linux!")
```

Resource Management

Efficient resource management involves loading and unloading assets based on platform capabilities. Techniques include:

- **Asset Bundling:** Bundling assets to reduce load times.
- **Lazy Loading:** Loading assets only when needed.
- **Memory Optimization:** Managing memory usage to prevent slowdowns.

Example: Lazy Loading

Here's an example of lazy loading assets:

```
class AssetManager:
    def __init__(self):
        self.assets = {}

    def get_asset(self, name):
        if name not in self.assets:
            self.assets[name] = self.load_asset(name)
        return self.assets[name]

    def load_asset(self, name):
        # Simulate loading asset
        print(f"Loading asset: {name}")
        return f"Asset({name})"

asset_manager = AssetManager()
asset = asset_manager.get_asset("texture.png")
print(asset)
```

Input Handling

Adapting input methods to the target platform ensures a seamless user experience. Techniques include:

- **Touch Controls:** Implementing touch controls for mobile platforms.
- **Gamepad Support:** Adding support for gamepads on consoles and PCs.
- **Keyboard and Mouse:** Optimizing keyboard and mouse input for PC platforms.

Example: Touch Controls

Here's an example of implementing touch controls for a mobile platform:

```
import pygame

pygame.init()
screen = pygame.display.set_mode((800, 600))
running = True

while running:
    for event in pygame.event.get():
        if event.type == pygame.QUIT:
            running = False
        elif event.type == pygame.FINGERDOWN:
            x, y = event.x * screen.get_width(), event.y * screen.get_height()
            print(f"Touch at ({x}, {y})")

    screen.fill((0, 0, 0))
    pygame.display.flip()

pygame.quit()
```

Performance Profiling

Profiling and optimizing performance for each platform ensures that the game runs smoothly. Techniques include:

- **Platform-Specific Profiling Tools:** Using tools like Xcode Instruments for iOS, Android Profiler for Android, and Visual Studio Profiler for Windows.
- **Benchmarking:** Running performance benchmarks on each platform to identify bottlenecks.
- **Optimization:** Applying platform-specific optimizations based on profiling results.

Example: Platform-Specific Profiling Tools

Here's an example of using platform-specific profiling tools:

- **iOS:** Xcode Instruments for profiling and optimizing iOS games.
- **Android:** Android Profiler for monitoring CPU, memory, and network usage.
- **Windows:** Visual Studio Profiler for identifying performance bottlenecks.

Conclusion

Optimizing games for different platforms is essential for providing a consistent and enjoyable gaming experience. By using techniques like conditional compilation, efficient resource management, adaptable input handling, and platform-specific performance profiling, developers can ensure that their games run smoothly across various devices and operating systems.

Conclusion

Enhancing game performance involves a combination of profiling, optimization, and platform-specific techniques. By understanding the unique challenges and opportunities presented by different platforms and applying efficient rendering strategies, developers can create high-performance games that provide a smooth and enjoyable experience for players across various devices and operating systems.

Chapter 13: Implementing Game UI

Designing User Interfaces

Designing user interfaces (UI) is a critical aspect of game development. A well-designed UI enhances player experience, providing intuitive access to game features and information. When designing a UI, consider the following principles:

1. **Consistency:** Ensure that UI elements behave and look consistent throughout the game. Consistent buttons, fonts, and layouts help players quickly understand and navigate the interface.

2. **Simplicity:** Keep the UI simple and uncluttered. Avoid overwhelming players with too much information or too many options at once. Use clear and concise labels and icons.

3. **Feedback:** Provide immediate and clear feedback for player actions. This can be visual (like button animations), auditory (sound effects), or tactile (vibration).

4. **Accessibility:** Make your UI accessible to all players, including those with disabilities. Consider using larger fonts, high-contrast colors, and providing options for colorblind players.

5. **Usability Testing:** Regularly test your UI with real users to identify issues and gather feedback. This iterative process helps refine the UI to better meet player needs.

In PyGame, you can create UI elements using various methods, including custom drawing functions and third-party libraries like `pygame_gui`. Here is an example of creating a simple button using PyGame:

```python
import pygame

pygame.init()
screen = pygame.display.set_mode((800, 600))

# Define colors
WHITE = (255, 255, 255)
BLUE = (0, 0, 255)

# Button properties
button_rect = pygame.Rect(300, 250, 200, 50)

running = True
while running:
```

```
        for event in pygame.event.get():
            if event.type == pygame.QUIT:
                running = False
            elif event.type == pygame.MOUSEBUTTONDOWN:
                if button_rect.collidepoint(event.pos):
                    print("Button clicked!")

        screen.fill(WHITE)
        pygame.draw.rect(screen, BLUE, button_rect)
        pygame.display.flip()

pygame.quit()
```

This code creates a simple window with a clickable button. When the button is clicked, a message is printed to the console.

Creating Menus and Buttons

Creating menus and buttons is essential for game navigation, allowing players to start the game, adjust settings, or exit. PyGame provides flexibility in designing custom menus and buttons.

To create a menu, you can define a series of buttons and their respective actions. Below is an example of a simple main menu with start and quit options:

```
import pygame
import sys

pygame.init()
screen = pygame.display.set_mode((800, 600))
font = pygame.font.Font(None, 74)

def draw_text(text, font, color, surface, x, y):
    text_obj = font.render(text, True, color)
    text_rect = text_obj.get_rect()
    text_rect.center = (x, y)
    surface.blit(text_obj, text_rect)

def main_menu():
    while True:
        screen.fill((0, 0, 0))
```

```
        draw_text('Main Menu', font, (255, 255, 255), screen, 400,
100)

        mx, my = pygame.mouse.get_pos()
        button_start = pygame.Rect(300, 200, 200, 50)
        button_quit = pygame.Rect(300, 300, 200, 50)

        if button_start.collidepoint((mx, my)):
            if click:
                game()
        if button_quit.collidepoint((mx, my)):
            if click:
                pygame.quit()
                sys.exit()

        pygame.draw.rect(screen, (0, 0, 255), button_start)
        draw_text('Start', font, (255, 255, 255), screen, 400, 225)
        pygame.draw.rect(screen, (255, 0, 0), button_quit)
        draw_text('Quit', font, (255, 255, 255), screen, 400, 325)

        click = False
        for event in pygame.event.get():
            if event.type == pygame.QUIT:
                pygame.quit()
                sys.exit()
            if event.type == pygame.MOUSEBUTTONDOWN:
                if event.button == 1:
                    click = True

        pygame.display.update()

def game():
    running = True
    while running:
        for event in pygame.event.get():
            if event.type == pygame.QUIT:
                pygame.quit()
                sys.exit()

        screen.fill((0, 0, 0))
```

```
        draw_text('Game Screen', font, (255, 255, 255), screen, 400,
300)
        pygame.display.update()

main_menu()
```

This code demonstrates a main menu with "Start" and "Quit" buttons. Clicking "Start" transitions to the game screen, while "Quit" exits the application.

Integrating UI with Game Logic

Integrating UI with game logic ensures that UI elements interact correctly with the game's state and mechanics. This integration involves updating UI elements based on game events and vice versa.

For example, if your game has a score system, you need to display the score on the screen and update it as the player progresses. Here's how you can integrate a score display with the game logic:

```
import pygame

pygame.init()
screen = pygame.display.set_mode((800, 600))
font = pygame.font.Font(None, 74)

score = 0

def draw_text(text, font, color, surface, x, y):
    text_obj = font.render(text, True, color)
    text_rect = text_obj.get_rect()
    text_rect.center = (x, y)
    surface.blit(text_obj, text_rect)

running = True
while running:
    for event in pygame.event.get():
        if event.type == pygame.QUIT:
            running = False
        if event.type == pygame.KEYDOWN:
            if event.key == pygame.K_SPACE:
                score += 10
```

```
    screen.fill((0, 0, 0))
    draw_text(f'Score: {score}', font, (255, 255, 255), screen, 400,
50)
    pygame.display.flip()

pygame.quit()
```

In this example, pressing the space bar increases the score by 10, and the updated score is displayed on the screen.

Responsive UI Design

Responsive UI design ensures that your game's UI adapts to different screen sizes and resolutions. This is crucial for providing a consistent user experience across various devices.

To create a responsive UI in PyGame, you can use relative positioning and scaling for UI elements. Here's an example of how to create a responsive button:

```
import pygame

pygame.init()
screen = pygame.display.set_mode((0, 0), pygame.FULLSCREEN)
screen_width, screen_height = screen.get_size()

WHITE = (255, 255, 255)
BLUE = (0, 0, 255)

button_width = int(screen_width * 0.25)
button_height = int(screen_height * 0.1)
button_x = (screen_width - button_width) // 2
button_y = (screen_height - button_height) // 2
button_rect   =   pygame.Rect(button_x,   button_y,   button_width,
button_height)

running = True
while running:
    for event in pygame.event.get():
        if event.type == pygame.QUIT:
            running = False
        elif event.type == pygame.MOUSEBUTTONDOWN:
```

```
            if button_rect.collidepoint(event.pos):
                print("Button clicked!")

    screen.fill(WHITE)
    pygame.draw.rect(screen, BLUE, button_rect)
    pygame.display.flip()

pygame.quit()
```

In this code, the button's size and position are calculated relative to the screen size, ensuring it scales appropriately on different devices.

User Experience Testing

User experience (UX) testing involves evaluating the game's UI and overall usability by observing real users interacting with the game. This process helps identify pain points and areas for improvement.

1. Plan Testing Sessions: Define the goals and scope of your testing sessions. Identify specific tasks or scenarios for users to complete.

2. Recruit Testers: Find a diverse group of testers that represents your target audience. Include both experienced gamers and novices to get a broad perspective.

3. Conduct Testing: Observe users as they interact with your game. Take notes on their behavior, struggles, and feedback. Avoid guiding them too much, as independent interactions provide the most valuable insights.

4. Analyze Results: Compile and analyze the feedback and observations. Identify common issues and prioritize them based on their impact on the user experience.

5. Iterate and Improve: Make necessary adjustments to the UI and game mechanics based on the feedback. Repeat the testing process to validate the changes and continue refining the game.

By regularly conducting UX testing, you ensure that your game's UI is user-friendly and meets player expectations, ultimately leading to a more enjoyable gaming experience.

Chapter 14: Advanced Graphics Techniques

Working with 2D Graphics

Working with 2D graphics involves creating and manipulating images, sprites, and visual effects to enhance the visual appeal of your game. PyGame provides various tools and functions to handle 2D graphics efficiently.

1. Loading and Displaying Images: PyGame allows you to load images from files and display them on the screen. Use `pygame.image.load()` to load an image and `blit()` to draw it.

```python
import pygame

pygame.init()
screen = pygame.display.set_mode((800, 600))
background = pygame.image.load('background.png')

running = True
while running:
    for event in pygame.event.get():
        if event.type == pygame.QUIT:
            running = False

    screen.blit(background, (0, 0))
    pygame.display.flip()

pygame.quit()
```

2. Sprite Sheets: Sprite sheets are used to store multiple images in a single file, which can be used for animations and managing multiple sprites efficiently.

```python
class SpriteSheet:
    def __init__(self, filename):
        self.sheet = pygame.image.load(filename).convert()

    def get_image(self, x, y, width, height):
```

```python
            image = pygame.Surface((width, height)).convert()
            image.blit(self.sheet, (0, 0), (x, y, width, height))
            image.set_colorkey((0, 0, 0))
            return image

sprite_sheet = SpriteSheet('spritesheet.png')
sprite = sprite_sheet.get_image(0, 0, 32, 32)
```

3. Animations: Creating animations involves displaying a sequence of images over time. Use sprite sheets to organize your animation frames.

```python
class Player(pygame.sprite.Sprite):
    def __init__(self):
        super().__init__()
        self.images = []
        self.images.append(pygame.image.load('frame_1.png'))
        self.images.append(pygame.image.load('frame_2.png'))
        self.index = 0
        self.image = self.images[self.index]
        self.rect = self.image.get_rect()

    def update(self):
        self.index += 1
        if self.index >= len(self.images):
            self.index = 0
        self.image = self.images[self.index]

player = Player()
all_sprites = pygame.sprite.Group()
all_sprites.add(player)

running = True
while running:
    for event in pygame.event.get():
        if event.type == pygame.QUIT:
            running = False

    all_sprites.update()
    screen.fill((0, 0, 0))
    all_sprites.draw(screen)
    pygame.display.flip()
```

```
pygame.quit()
```

4. **Applying Transformations:** Transformations such as scaling, rotating, and flipping images can be performed using PyGame's transformation functions.

```
image = pygame.image.load('sprite.png')
scaled_image = pygame.transform.scale(image, (64, 64))
rotated_image = pygame.transform.rotate(image, 45)
flipped_image = pygame.transform.flip(image, True, False)
```

Introduction to 3D Graphics in PyGame

While PyGame is primarily a 2D library, it is possible to create 3D effects using techniques like isometric projection and pseudo-3D rendering.

1. **Isometric Projection:** Isometric projection simulates 3D by representing 3D objects in 2D space. This technique is commonly used in strategy and simulation games.

```
def iso_coords(x, y):
    iso_x = x - y
    iso_y = (x + y) / 2
    return iso_x, iso_y


tile_width = 64
tile_height = 32

for x in range(10):
    for y in range(10):
        iso_x, iso_y = iso_coords(x * tile_width, y * tile_height)
        pygame.draw.polygon(screen, (0, 255, 0), [(iso_x, iso_y), (iso_x + tile_width / 2, iso_y + tile_height / 2), (iso_x, iso_y + tile_height), (iso_x - tile_width / 2, iso_y + tile_height / 2)])
```

2. **Pseudo-3D Rendering:** Pseudo-3D techniques, such as ray casting, create the illusion of 3D in a 2D environment. This approach was famously used in early first-person shooters like Wolfenstein 3D.

```
import math
```

```python
class RayCaster:
    def __init__(self, map, screen):
        self.map = map
        self.screen = screen
        self.width = screen.get_width()
        self.height = screen.get_height()

    def cast_ray(self, angle):
        # Ray casting logic here
        pass

    def render(self, player_pos, player_angle):
        for x in range(self.width):
            ray_angle = player_angle + (x / self.width - 0.5) * math.pi / 3
            self.cast_ray(ray_angle)

ray_caster = RayCaster(map, screen)
ray_caster.render(player_pos, player_angle)
```

Shaders and Special Effects

Shaders are programs that run on the GPU, allowing for advanced graphical effects. While PyGame does not natively support shaders, you can use libraries like PyOpenGL to integrate shader functionality.

1. Introduction to Shaders: Shaders are written in languages like GLSL and are used to control the rendering pipeline. Vertex shaders manipulate vertex data, while fragment shaders handle pixel colors.

2. Implementing Shaders with PyOpenGL: To use shaders in PyGame, first install PyOpenGL:

```
pip install PyOpenGL
```

Then, create and compile shader programs:

```python
from OpenGL.GL import *
from OpenGL.GL.shaders import compileProgram, compileShader
```

```
vertex_shader_source = """
#version 330
layout(location = 0) in vec3 position;
void main() {
    gl_Position = vec4(position, 1.0);
}
"""

fragment_shader_source = """
#version 330
out vec4 fragColor;
void main() {
    fragColor = vec4(1.0, 0.0, 0.0, 1.0);
}
"""

shader_program = compileProgram(
    compileShader(vertex_shader_source, GL_VERTEX_SHADER),
    compileShader(fragment_shader_source, GL_FRAGMENT_SHADER)
)
glUseProgram(shader_program)
```

3. **Applying Shaders:** Use the compiled shader program to render objects with special effects. This example renders a red triangle:

```
vertices = [
    -0.5, -0.5, 0.0,
     0.5, -0.5, 0.0,
     0.0,  0.5, 0.0
]

vao = glGenVertexArrays(1)
vbo = glGenBuffers(1)
glBindVertexArray(vao)

glBindBuffer(GL_ARRAY_BUFFER, vbo)
glBufferData(GL_ARRAY_BUFFER, np.array(vertices, dtype=np.float32), GL_STATIC_DRAW)

glVertexAttribPointer(0, 3, GL_FLOAT, GL_FALSE, 0, None)
```

```
glEnableVertexAttribArray(0)

glBindBuffer(GL_ARRAY_BUFFER, 0)
glBindVertexArray(0)

running = True
while running:
    for event in pygame.event.get():
        if event.type == pygame.QUIT:
            running = False

    glClear(GL_COLOR_BUFFER_BIT)
    glBindVertexArray(vao)
    glDrawArrays(GL_TRIANGLES, 0, 3)
    pygame.display.flip()

pygame.quit()
```

Lighting and Shadows

Lighting and shadows add realism and depth to game graphics. Implementing these effects can be complex, but it greatly enhances the visual experience.

1. Basic Lighting: Simulate simple lighting effects by adjusting the brightness of sprites based on their position relative to a light source.

```
def apply_lighting(image, light_pos):
    width, height = image.get_size()
    for x in range(width):
        for y in range(height):
            pixel_color = image.get_at((x, y))
            distance = math.hypot(light_pos[0] - x, light_pos[1] - y)
            brightness = max(0, 255 - int(distance))
            pixel_color = (brightness, brightness, brightness)
            image.set_at((x, y), pixel_color)
```

2. Dynamic Shadows: Create dynamic shadows by casting rays from the light source to detect obstacles and shade the area accordingly.

```python
def cast_shadow(light_pos, obstacles):
    for obstacle in obstacles:
        shadow_vertices = calculate_shadow_vertices(light_pos, obstacle)
        pygame.draw.polygon(screen, (0, 0, 0), shadow_vertices)
```

3. Advanced Lighting with Shaders: Use shaders for more advanced lighting effects, including point lights, spotlights, and global illumination.

```
#version 330

in vec3 FragPos;
in vec3 Normal;
out vec4 FragColor;

uniform vec3 lightPos;
uniform vec3 viewPos;
uniform vec3 lightColor;
uniform vec3 objectColor;

void main() {
    float ambientStrength = 0.1;
    vec3 ambient = ambientStrength * lightColor;

    vec3 norm = normalize(Normal);
    vec3 lightDir = normalize(lightPos - FragPos);
    float diff = max(dot(norm, lightDir), 0.0);
    vec3 diffuse = diff * lightColor;

    float specularStrength = 0.5;
    vec3 viewDir = normalize(viewPos - FragPos);
    vec3 reflectDir = reflect(-lightDir, norm);
    float spec = pow(max(dot(viewDir, reflectDir), 0.0), 32);
    vec3 specular = specularStrength * spec * lightColor;

    vec3 result = (ambient + diffuse + specular) * objectColor;
    FragColor = vec4(result, 1.0);
}
```

Procedural Content Generation

Procedural content generation (PCG) creates game content algorithmically, reducing the need for manually crafted assets. PCG can be used for generating levels, landscapes, textures, and more.

1. **Random Level Generation:** Create levels using random algorithms. For example, generate a maze using depth-first search.

```
def generate_maze(width, height):
    maze = [[0 for _ in range(width)] for _ in range(height)]
    stack = [(0, 0)]
    while stack:
        x, y = stack.pop()
        maze[y][x] = 1
        neighbors = get_unvisited_neighbors(x, y, maze)
        if neighbors:
            stack.append((x, y))
            nx, ny = random.choice(neighbors)
            remove_wall(x, y, nx, ny, maze)
            stack.append((nx, ny))
    return maze
```

2. **Perlin Noise for Landscapes:** Use Perlin noise to generate natural-looking terrain and landscapes.

```
import noise

def generate_terrain(width, height, scale=100):
    terrain = [[0 for _ in range(width)] for _ in range(height)]
    for y in range(height):
        for x in range(width):
            terrain[y][x] = noise.pnoise2(x / scale, y / scale)
    return terrain
```

3. **Procedural Textures:** Generate textures programmatically using algorithms like Voronoi diagrams and fractals.

```
def generate_voronoi(width, height, num_cells):
```

```
    points = [(random.randint(0, width), random.randint(0, height)) 
for _ in range(num_cells)]
    voronoi = [[0 for _ in range(width)] for _ in range(height)]
    for y in range(height):
        for x in range(width):
            distances = [math.hypot(px - x, py - y) for px, py in points]
            voronoi[y][x] = distances.index(min(distances))
    return voronoi
```

By leveraging these advanced graphics techniques, you can create visually stunning and engaging games with PyGame.

Chapter 15: Building a Game Engine

Understanding Game Engines

Building a game engine is a complex but rewarding task. A game engine is a software framework designed to facilitate the development of video games. It provides a suite of tools and capabilities that help developers create games efficiently. Understanding the core components and architecture of a game engine is crucial for creating robust and high-performance games.

A game engine typically includes the following components:

- **Rendering Engine**: Handles the graphics rendering, including 2D and 3D graphics.
- **Physics Engine**: Manages the physics simulations, such as collision detection and response, gravity, and other physical interactions.
- **Audio Engine**: Provides support for sound effects and music.
- **Input System**: Handles user input from devices like keyboards, mice, gamepads, and touchscreens.
- **Scripting Engine**: Allows developers to write game logic and behaviors in a high-level scripting language.
- **Animation System**: Manages animations for characters and other in-game objects.
- **Artificial Intelligence (AI)**: Provides tools for creating non-player characters (NPCs) and other intelligent behaviors.
- **Networking**: Supports multiplayer features and online interactions.
- **Memory Management**: Ensures efficient use of memory and resources.
- **Debugging and Profiling Tools**: Help identify and fix performance issues and bugs.

Understanding these components and how they interact is the first step in designing your game engine.

Core Components of a Game Engine

When building a game engine, it's essential to design and implement the core components effectively. These components form the backbone of your engine and determine its capabilities and performance.

Rendering Engine

The rendering engine is responsible for drawing graphics on the screen. It handles everything from simple 2D sprites to complex 3D models and scenes. The rendering engine needs to be efficient and capable of handling a large number of objects smoothly.

```
import pygame
from pygame.locals import *
```

```
pygame.init()

# Set up the display
screen = pygame.display.set_mode((800, 600))

# Main loop
running = True
while running:
    for event in pygame.event.get():
        if event.type == QUIT:
            running = False

        # Clear the screen
        screen.fill((0, 0, 0))

        # Draw something (e.g., a rectangle)
        pygame.draw.rect(screen, (255, 0, 0), (100, 100, 200, 100))

        # Update the display
        pygame.display.flip()

pygame.quit()
```

Physics Engine

The physics engine simulates physical interactions in the game world. This includes gravity, collisions, and other forces. A robust physics engine is crucial for creating realistic and engaging gameplay.

Audio Engine

The audio engine handles sound effects and music. It should support multiple audio formats and provide features like volume control, audio panning, and 3D spatial sound.

Input System

The input system processes user inputs from various devices. It needs to be responsive and capable of handling multiple inputs simultaneously.

Scripting Engine

The scripting engine allows developers to write game logic in a high-level scripting language. This makes it easier to implement and modify game behaviors without changing the core engine code.

Animation System

The animation system manages character and object animations. It should support keyframe animations, skeletal animations, and other techniques to bring your game to life.

Artificial Intelligence (AI)

The AI component provides tools for creating intelligent behaviors for NPCs and other game elements. This includes pathfinding, decision-making, and other AI techniques.

Networking

The networking component supports multiplayer features and online interactions. It should handle data synchronization, latency management, and other networking challenges.

Memory Management

Efficient memory management is crucial for maintaining performance. The engine should manage resources like textures, models, and sounds effectively to avoid memory leaks and performance issues.

Debugging and Profiling Tools

Debugging and profiling tools help identify and fix performance issues and bugs. They provide insights into how the engine is performing and where optimizations are needed.

Designing Your Engine Architecture

Designing the architecture of your game engine involves planning how the different components will interact and work together. A well-designed architecture ensures that your engine is flexible, modular, and scalable.

Modular Design

A modular design approach breaks down the engine into independent components or modules. Each module handles a specific aspect of the engine's functionality, making it easier to develop, test, and maintain.

Component-Based Architecture

A component-based architecture focuses on creating reusable components that can be combined to build game objects. This approach promotes code reuse and flexibility.

Entity-Component-System (ECS)

The ECS pattern is a popular architecture for game engines. It separates game objects (entities) from their data (components) and behavior (systems). This separation makes it easier to manage and optimize game objects.

Event-Driven Architecture

An event-driven architecture uses events to trigger actions in the engine. This approach decouples different parts of the engine, making it more modular and easier to extend.

Data-Driven Design

Data-driven design involves using external data files to define game content and behavior. This approach makes it easier to modify and extend the game without changing the engine code.

Implementing Engine Features

Once you have designed your engine architecture, the next step is to implement the core features. This involves writing the code for each component and ensuring they work together seamlessly.

Rendering

Start by implementing the rendering engine. This involves setting up the graphics context, loading assets, and drawing objects on the screen.

Physics

Next, implement the physics engine. This includes defining physical properties, handling collisions, and simulating forces.

Audio

Implement the audio engine to handle sound effects and music. This involves loading audio files, playing sounds, and managing audio channels.

Input

Implement the input system to handle user inputs from various devices. This includes processing keyboard, mouse, and gamepad inputs.

Scripting

Add the scripting engine to allow developers to write game logic. Choose a scripting language that is easy to integrate and use.

Animation

Implement the animation system to manage character and object animations. This involves loading animation data and updating the animation states.

AI

Implement the AI component to create intelligent behaviors for NPCs. This includes pathfinding, decision-making, and other AI techniques.

Networking

Add the networking component to support multiplayer features. This involves handling data synchronization, latency management, and other networking challenges.

Memory Management

Implement memory management techniques to ensure efficient use of resources. This includes managing textures, models, and sounds.

Debugging and Profiling

Add debugging and profiling tools to identify and fix performance issues. These tools provide insights into the engine's performance and help optimize the code.

Testing and Debugging Your Engine

Testing and debugging are crucial steps in building a game engine. This involves thoroughly testing each component and ensuring they work together as expected.

Unit Testing

Write unit tests for each component to ensure they work correctly in isolation. This helps catch bugs early and makes it easier to debug issues.

Integration Testing

Perform integration testing to ensure the different components work together seamlessly. This involves testing the interactions between components and verifying the overall functionality of the engine.

Performance Testing

Conduct performance testing to identify and fix performance bottlenecks. This involves profiling the engine and optimizing code to ensure smooth gameplay.

User Testing

User testing involves having real users test the engine and provide feedback. This helps identify usability issues and ensures the engine meets the needs of developers.

Continuous Integration

Set up continuous integration (CI) to automate the testing process. This involves running tests automatically whenever changes are made to the codebase, ensuring the engine remains stable and reliable.

Core Components of a Game Engine

The core components of a game engine are the essential building blocks that provide the foundation for game development. Understanding and implementing these components effectively is crucial for creating a robust and efficient game engine. The main core components include:

Rendering Engine

The rendering engine is responsible for drawing all the visuals in the game. It handles the rendering of 2D sprites, 3D models, textures, and shaders. A good rendering engine must be optimized for performance, supporting high frame rates and smooth graphics. It should also be flexible, allowing for easy integration of new graphical features.

Physics Engine

The physics engine simulates the physical interactions in the game world. This includes gravity, collision detection, and response, as well as more complex simulations like ragdoll physics and fluid dynamics. A robust physics engine enhances the realism of the game and is essential for games that rely heavily on physical interactions.

Audio Engine

The audio engine manages all the sound effects and music in the game. It should support various audio formats and provide features like 3D positional audio, volume control, and audio mixing. An effective audio engine adds to the immersion of the game by providing high-quality and well-timed sound effects.

Input System

The input system handles all the user inputs from devices like keyboards, mice, gamepads, and touchscreens. It needs to be responsive and capable of processing multiple inputs simultaneously. A well-designed input system is crucial for creating a smooth and responsive gameplay experience.

Scripting Engine

The scripting engine allows developers to write game logic and behaviors using a high-level scripting language. This makes it easier to implement and modify game mechanics without having to change the core engine code. Popular scripting languages for game engines include Lua, Python, and JavaScript.

Animation System

The animation system manages the animations of characters and objects in the game. It should support various animation techniques like keyframe animation, skeletal animation, and blend trees. A robust animation system brings the game world to life by providing smooth and realistic animations.

Networking

The networking component handles all the online and multiplayer features of the game. It manages data synchronization between clients and servers, handles latency issues, and ensures a smooth online experience. A good networking component is essential for multiplayer games.

Memory Management

Memory management is crucial for ensuring that the game runs efficiently without crashing or slowing down. The engine should manage the allocation and deallocation of memory for game assets like textures, models, and sounds. Proper memory management prevents memory leaks and optimizes the use of system resources.

Debugging Tools

Debugging tools help developers identify and fix bugs and performance issues in the game engine. These tools can include loggers, profilers, and visual debuggers. Effective debugging tools are essential for maintaining the stability and performance of the game engine.

Designing Your Engine Architecture

Designing the architecture of your game engine involves defining how the core components will interact and work together. A well-designed architecture is crucial for creating a flexible, modular, and scalable engine. Key architectural patterns and principles to consider include:

Modular Design

Modular design involves breaking down the engine into independent modules that can be developed, tested, and maintained separately. This approach makes it easier to add new features and update existing ones without affecting other parts of the engine.

Component-Based Architecture

A component-based architecture uses entities and components to represent game objects. Each entity is a container for components that define its behavior and properties. This approach promotes code reuse and flexibility, making it easier to create complex game objects.

Event-Driven Architecture

Event-driven architecture uses events to communicate between different parts of the engine. This decouples the components and allows them to interact without direct dependencies. Event-driven systems are flexible and scalable, making it easier to add new features and handle complex interactions.

Data-Driven Design

Data-driven design involves using external data files to define game content and behavior. This approach makes it easier to update and modify the game without changing the engine code. Data-driven design is particularly useful for defining game levels, character stats, and other configurable elements.

Entity-Component-System (ECS) Pattern

The ECS pattern is a popular architecture for game engines. It separates the data (components) from the behavior (systems) and uses entities to organize the components. This separation makes it easier to manage and optimize the game objects, improving performance and flexibility.

Implementing Engine Features

Implementing the features of your game engine involves writing the code for each core component and ensuring they work together seamlessly. This section provides an overview of the implementation process for the main features of a game engine.

Rendering Engine

Start by implementing the rendering engine. This involves setting up the graphics context, loading assets, and drawing objects on the screen. You can use libraries like OpenGL, DirectX, or Vulkan for low-level graphics programming, or higher-level libraries like SDL or SFML for easier integration.

Physics Engine

Next, implement the physics engine. This includes defining physical properties, handling collisions, and simulating forces like gravity and friction. You can use physics libraries like Box2D or Bullet to handle the complex mathematics and algorithms required for realistic physics simulations.

Audio Engine

Implement the audio engine to handle sound effects and music. This involves loading audio files, playing sounds, and managing audio channels. Libraries like OpenAL or FMOD provide powerful tools for audio programming.

Input System

Implement the input system to handle user inputs from various devices. This includes processing keyboard, mouse, and gamepad inputs, and mapping them to game actions. Libraries like SDL or GLFW can help with input handling.

Scripting Engine

Add the scripting engine to allow developers to write game logic. Choose a scripting language that is easy to integrate and use, such as Lua, Python, or JavaScript. Implement a scripting interface that allows the scripts to interact with the core engine components.

Animation System

Implement the animation system to manage character and object animations. This involves loading animation data, updating the animation states, and blending animations for smooth transitions. You can use libraries like Spine or Spriter for advanced animation features.

AI

Implement the AI component to create intelligent behaviors for NPCs. This includes pathfinding, decision-making, and other AI techniques. Libraries like A* Pathfinding or Behavior Trees can help with AI implementation.

Networking

Add the networking component to support multiplayer features. This involves handling data synchronization, latency management, and other networking challenges. Libraries like ENet or RakNet provide tools for building reliable networked games.

Memory Management

Implement memory management techniques to ensure efficient use of resources. This includes managing textures, models, and sounds, and preventing memory leaks. Use smart pointers and other memory management tools to automate resource management.

Debugging and Profiling

Add debugging and profiling tools to identify and fix performance issues. These tools provide insights into the engine's performance and help optimize the code. Libraries like gDEBugger or Intel VTune can help with debugging and profiling.

Testing and Debugging Your Engine

Testing and debugging are crucial steps in building a game engine. This involves thoroughly testing each component and ensuring they work together as expected. Key testing and debugging techniques include:

Unit Testing

Write unit tests for each component to ensure they work correctly in isolation. This helps catch bugs early and makes it easier to debug issues. Use testing frameworks like Google Test or Catch2 for automated unit testing.

Integration Testing

Perform integration testing to ensure the different components work together seamlessly. This involves testing the interactions between components and verifying the overall functionality of the engine. Integration tests help identify issues that arise from component interactions.

Performance Testing

Conduct performance testing to identify and fix performance bottlenecks. This involves profiling the engine and optimizing code to ensure smooth gameplay. Tools like Visual Studio Profiler or Valgrind can help with performance testing.

User Testing

User testing involves having real users test the engine and provide feedback. This helps identify usability issues and ensures the engine meets the needs of developers. Collect feedback from users and iterate on the engine design based on their input.

Continuous Integration

Set up continuous integration (CI) to automate the testing process. This involves running tests automatically whenever changes are made to the codebase, ensuring the engine remains stable and reliable. Use CI tools like Jenkins or Travis CI for automated testing and deployment.

Implementing Engine Features

Implementing the features of a game engine is a complex and iterative process that requires careful planning and execution. Here are the steps involved in implementing the core features of a game engine:

Rendering Engine

The rendering engine is the heart of the game engine. It is responsible for drawing everything on the screen. To implement the rendering engine, you need to:

1. **Initialize the Graphics Context**: Set up the graphics context using libraries like OpenGL, DirectX, or Vulkan.
2. **Load Assets**: Load textures, models, and other graphical assets.
3. **Draw Objects**: Implement functions to draw objects on the screen.
4. **Optimize Rendering**: Use techniques like frustum culling, occlusion culling, and level of detail (LOD) to optimize rendering performance.

Here is an example of setting up a basic rendering loop using Pygame:

```
import pygame
from pygame.locals import *

pygame.init()

# Set up the display
screen = pygame.display.set_mode((800, 600))

# Main loop
running = True
while running:
    for event in pygame.event.get():
        if event.type == QUIT:
            running = False

    # Clear the screen
    screen.fill((0, 0, 0))

    # Draw something (e.g., a rectangle)
    pygame.draw.rect(screen, (255, 0, 0), (100, 100, 200, 100))

    # Update the display
    pygame.display.flip()

pygame.quit()
```

Physics Engine

The physics engine simulates physical interactions in the game world. To implement the physics engine, you need to:

1. **Define Physical Properties**: Define properties like mass, velocity, and acceleration for game objects.

2. **Implement Collision Detection**: Use algorithms like Axis-Aligned Bounding Box (AABB) or Separating Axis Theorem (SAT) for collision detection.
3. **Simulate Forces**: Implement functions to simulate forces like gravity, friction, and momentum.
4. **Handle Collisions**: Implement collision response to determine what happens when objects collide.

Audio Engine

The audio engine handles sound effects and music. To implement the audio engine, you need to:

1. **Load Audio Files**: Load sound effects and music files in various formats.
2. **Play Sounds**: Implement functions to play, pause, and stop sounds.
3. **Manage Audio Channels**: Manage multiple audio channels for simultaneous sound playback.
4. **Implement 3D Audio**: Simulate 3D audio effects for immersive sound experiences.

Input System

The input system handles user inputs from various devices. To implement the input system, you need to:

1. **Process Input Events**: Capture input events from devices like keyboards, mice, and gamepads.
2. **Map Inputs to Actions**: Map input events to game actions (e.g., moving a character, firing a weapon).
3. **Handle Multiple Inputs**: Ensure the system can handle multiple inputs simultaneously.
4. **Provide Input Feedback**: Implement feedback mechanisms like vibration for gamepads.

Scripting Engine

The scripting engine allows developers to write game logic. To implement the scripting engine, you need to:

1. **Choose a Scripting Language**: Select a scripting language like Lua, Python, or JavaScript.
2. **Integrate the Scripting Language**: Embed the scripting language in the engine and expose engine functions to the scripts.
3. **Execute Scripts**: Implement a runtime environment for executing scripts.
4. **Handle Script Errors**: Provide mechanisms for error handling and debugging in scripts.

Animation System

The animation system manages character and object animations. To implement the animation system, you need to:

1. **Load Animation Data**: Load animation data from files.
2. **Update Animation States**: Implement functions to update the animation states of objects.
3. **Blend Animations**: Provide blending techniques for smooth transitions between animations.
4. **Optimize Animation Performance**: Use techniques like keyframe reduction and hardware skinning to optimize performance.

AI

The AI component creates intelligent behaviors for NPCs. To implement the AI component, you need to:

1. **Implement Pathfinding**: Use algorithms like A* for pathfinding.
2. **Define Behavior Trees**: Use behavior trees or finite state machines to define NPC behaviors.
3. **Implement Decision-Making**: Provide mechanisms for NPCs to make decisions based on game states.
4. **Simulate Group Behaviors**: Implement techniques for group behaviors like flocking and formations.

Networking

The networking component supports multiplayer features. To implement the networking component, you need to:

1. **Set Up Server-Client Architecture**: Design the architecture for server-client communication.
2. **Synchronize Game States**: Ensure game states are synchronized across clients and the server.
3. **Handle Latency**: Implement techniques to handle network latency and ensure a smooth experience.
4. **Provide Security**: Implement security measures to prevent cheating and protect player data.

Memory Management

Memory management ensures efficient use of resources. To implement memory management, you need to:

1. **Manage Resource Allocation**: Implement functions for allocating and deallocating resources.
2. **Prevent Memory Leaks**: Use tools and techniques to detect and prevent memory leaks.

3. **Optimize Resource Usage**: Optimize the use of textures, models, and sounds to reduce memory footprint.
4. **Implement Garbage Collection**: Use garbage collection mechanisms to manage memory automatically.

Debugging and Profiling

Debugging and profiling tools help identify and fix issues. To implement debugging and profiling tools, you need to:

1. **Provide Logging**: Implement logging mechanisms to capture and record engine events.
2. **Profile Performance**: Use profiling tools to measure performance and identify bottlenecks.
3. **Implement Breakpoints**: Provide mechanisms for setting breakpoints and inspecting game states.
4. **Visualize Data**: Use visual debugging tools to visualize data like collision boxes, AI states, and performance metrics.

Testing and Debugging Your Engine

Testing and debugging are crucial steps in building a game engine. This involves thoroughly testing each component and ensuring they work together as expected. Key testing and debugging techniques include:

Unit Testing

Write unit tests for each component to ensure they work correctly in isolation. This helps catch bugs early and makes it easier to debug issues. Use testing frameworks like Google Test or Catch2 for automated unit testing.

Integration Testing

Perform integration testing to ensure the different components work together seamlessly. This involves testing the interactions between components and verifying the overall functionality of the engine. Integration tests help identify issues that arise from component interactions.

Performance Testing

Conduct performance testing to identify and fix performance bottlenecks. This involves profiling the engine and optimizing code to ensure smooth gameplay. Tools like Visual Studio Profiler or Valgrind can help with performance testing.

User Testing

User testing involves having real users test the engine and provide feedback. This helps identify usability issues and ensures the engine meets the needs of developers. Collect feedback from users and iterate on the engine design based on their input.

Continuous Integration

Set up continuous integration (CI) to automate the testing process. This involves running tests automatically whenever changes are made to the codebase, ensuring the engine remains stable and reliable. Use CI tools like Jenkins or Travis CI for automated testing and deployment.

Chapter 16: Integrating Third-Party Libraries

Overview of Useful Libraries

Integrating third-party libraries into your game engine can significantly enhance its capabilities and save development time. These libraries provide pre-built solutions for common problems, allowing you to focus on creating unique gameplay experiences. Here are some useful libraries to consider:

Pyglet

Pyglet is a cross-platform windowing and multimedia library for Python, providing support for OpenGL graphics, window management, and multimedia playback. It is lightweight and easy to use, making it an excellent choice for 2D and 3D games.

OpenGL

OpenGL is a powerful cross-platform graphics API used for rendering 2D and 3D graphics. It provides a wide range of features for creating high-performance graphics applications. Integrating OpenGL with your game engine allows you to leverage its advanced rendering capabilities.

Box2D

Box2D is a popular physics engine used in many games. It provides a robust framework for simulating 2D physics, including collision detection, rigid body dynamics, and joints. Integrating Box2D can save you the effort of writing your own physics engine.

FMOD

FMOD is a comprehensive audio engine that provides tools for playing and manipulating sound in games. It supports various audio formats and advanced features like 3D sound, DSP effects, and interactive music. FMOD is widely used in the gaming industry for its powerful and flexible audio capabilities.

TensorFlow

TensorFlow is an open-source machine learning library developed by Google. It provides tools for building and training machine learning models, which can be used to implement advanced AI features in your game, such as neural networks for NPC behavior.

SDL

Simple DirectMedia Layer (SDL) is a cross-platform development library that provides low-level access to audio, keyboard, mouse, and graphics hardware. It is often used as a foundation for game engines due to its simplicity and flexibility.

ImGui

Immediate Mode Graphical User Interface (ImGui) is a bloat-free graphical user interface library for C++. It is designed for creating tools and debug interfaces, making it a great addition to your engine for developing in-game editors and debugging tools.

Integrating with Pyglet and OpenGL

Integrating Pyglet and OpenGL into your game engine allows you to leverage powerful graphics capabilities for both 2D and 3D rendering. Here are the steps to integrate these libraries:

Setting Up Pyglet

To use Pyglet in your game engine, start by installing the library:

```
pip install pyglet
```

Next, create a basic Pyglet window to render graphics:

```python
import pyglet
from pyglet.gl import *

# Create a window
window = pyglet.window.Window(width=800, height=600, caption="My Game Engine")

@window.event
def on_draw():
    glClear(GL_COLOR_BUFFER_BIT)
    # Draw something here

# Run the Pyglet event loop
pyglet.app.run()
```

Integrating OpenGL

To integrate OpenGL with Pyglet, you can use OpenGL functions directly within the Pyglet window. Here's an example of rendering a simple 3D object:

```python
import pyglet
from pyglet.gl import *

window = pyglet.window.Window(width=800, height=600, caption="My Game Engine")

@window.event
def on_draw():
    glClear(GL_COLOR_BUFFER_BIT | GL_DEPTH_BUFFER_BIT)
    glLoadIdentity()
    # Draw a triangle
    glBegin(GL_TRIANGLES)
    glVertex3f(0.0, 1.0, 0.0)
    glVertex3f(-1.0, -1.0, 0.0)
    glVertex3f(1.0, -1.0, 0.0)
    glEnd()

pyglet.app.run()
```

Handling Input with Pyglet

Pyglet provides built-in support for handling user input. You can capture keyboard and mouse events using event handlers:

```python
@window.event
def on_key_press(symbol, modifiers):
    if symbol == pyglet.window.key.ESCAPE:
        pyglet.app.exit()

@window.event
def on_mouse_motion(x, y, dx, dy):
    print(f"Mouse moved to ({x}, {y})")

pyglet.app.run()
```

Loading Textures

Chapter 16: Integrating Third-Party Libraries

To load and use textures in Pyglet, you can use the `pyglet.image` module. Here's an example of loading and displaying a texture:

```
texture = pyglet.image.load('texture.png').get_texture()

@window.event
def on_draw():
    glClear(GL_COLOR_BUFFER_BIT)
    glEnable(texture.target)
    glBindTexture(texture.target, texture.id)
    glBegin(GL_QUADS)
    glTexCoord2f(0.0, 0.0)
    glVertex2f(100, 100)
    glTexCoord2f(1.0, 0.0)
    glVertex2f(200, 100)
    glTexCoord2f(1.0, 1.0)
    glVertex2f(200, 200)
    glTexCoord2f(0.0, 1.0)
    glVertex2f(100, 200)
    glEnd()
    glDisable(texture.target)

pyglet.app.run()
```

Implementing Advanced Features

With Pyglet and OpenGL integrated, you can implement advanced features like shaders, 3D models, and lighting. This requires knowledge of OpenGL programming and shader languages like GLSL.

Here's an example of using a simple vertex and fragment shader in OpenGL:

```
vertex_shader_source = """
#version 330 core
layout (location = 0) in vec3 aPos;

void main()
{
    gl_Position = vec4(aPos, 1.0);
}
"""
```

```
fragment_shader_source = """
#version 330 core
out vec4 FragColor;

void main()
{
    FragColor = vec4(1.0, 0.5, 0.2, 1.0);
}
"""

# Compile shaders and link program
def compile_shader(source, shader_type):
    shader = glCreateShader(shader_type)
    glShaderSource(shader, source)
    glCompileShader(shader)
    return shader

vertex_shader           =           compile_shader(vertex_shader_source,
GL_VERTEX_SHADER)
fragment_shader         =           compile_shader(fragment_shader_source,
GL_FRAGMENT_SHADER)
shader_program = glCreateProgram()
glAttachShader(shader_program, vertex_shader)
glAttachShader(shader_program, fragment_shader)
glLinkProgram(shader_program)

# Use the shader program
glUseProgram(shader_program)
```

Using Physics Libraries

Integrating a physics library like Box2D into your game engine allows you to simulate realistic physical interactions. Here are the steps to integrate Box2D:

Setting Up Box2D

First, install the Box2D library:

```
pip install box2d-py
```

Creating a Physics World

Create a physics world and add bodies to it:

```python
import Box2D
from Box2D.b2 import (world, polygonShape, staticBody, dynamicBody)

# Create the world
physics_world = world(gravity=(0, -10), doSleep=True)

# Create a static ground body
ground_body = physics_world.CreateStaticBody(
    position=(0, -10),
    shapes=polygonShape(box=(50, 10))
)

# Create a dynamic body
dynamic_body = physics_world.CreateDynamicBody(position=(0, 4))
dynamic_box   =   dynamic_body.CreatePolygonFixture(box=(1,   1), density=1, friction=0.3)
```

Simulating Physics

To simulate physics, step the physics world in the main loop:

```python
time_step = 1.0 / 60
vel_iters, pos_iters = 6, 2

while running:
    # Step the physics world
    physics_world.Step(time_step, vel_iters, pos_iters)
    physics_world.ClearForces()

    # Clear the screen
    screen.fill((0, 0, 0))

    # Draw the dynamic body
    for body in physics_world.bodies:
        for fixture in body.fixtures:
            shape = fixture.shape
```

```
            vertices = [(body.transform * v) * PPM for v in shape.vertices]
            vertices = [(v[0], SCREEN_HEIGHT - v[1]) for v in vertices]
            pygame.draw.polygon(screen, colors[body.type], vertices)

    pygame.display.flip()
    clock.tick(TARGET_FPS)
```

Handling Collisions

Box2D provides collision detection and response out of the box. You can handle collisions by defining contact listeners:

```
class ContactListener(Box2D.b2ContactListener):
    def BeginContact(self, contact):
        fixture_a, fixture_b = contact.fixtureA, contact.fixtureB
        print(f"Contact between {fixture_a.body.userData} and {fixture_b.body.userData}")

physics_world.contactListener = ContactListener()
```

Incorporating AI Libraries

Incorporating AI libraries into your game engine allows you to implement advanced AI behaviors. Here are some popular AI libraries and how to integrate them:

TensorFlow

TensorFlow can be used to implement neural networks for complex AI behaviors. Here's an example of training a simple neural network:

```
import tensorflow as tf
from tensorflow.keras.models import Sequential
from tensorflow.keras.layers import Dense

# Create a simple neural network
model = Sequential([
    Dense(128, activation='relu', input_shape=(input_dim,)),
    Dense(64, activation='relu'),
```

```python
    Dense(output_dim, activation='softmax')
])

model.compile(optimizer='adam',
loss='sparse_categorical_crossentropy', metrics=['accuracy'])

# Train the model
model.fit(train_data,            train_labels,            epochs=10,
validation_data=(val_data, val_labels))
```

Behavior Trees

Behavior trees are a popular AI technique for defining NPC behaviors. Libraries like `py_trees` provide tools for creating and managing behavior trees:

```python
import py_trees

# Define a simple behavior tree
root = py_trees.composites.Sequence("Root")
move    =    py_trees.behaviours.SetBlackboardVariable(name="Move",
variable_name="action", variable_value="move")
attack  =    py_trees.behaviours.SetBlackboardVariable(name="Attack",
variable_name="action", variable_value="attack")
root.add_children([move, attack])

# Create a blackboard and tick the tree
blackboard = py_trees.blackboard.Client(name="NPC")
root.tick_once()
print(blackboard.action)  # Output: move
```

Pathfinding

Pathfinding algorithms like A* can be implemented using libraries like `pathfinding`:

```python
from pathfinding.core.grid import Grid
from pathfinding.finder.a_star import AStarFinder

grid = Grid(matrix=[
    [0, 1, 0, 0, 0],
```

```
        [0, 1, 0, 1, 0],
        [0, 0, 0, 1, 0],
        [0, 1, 1, 1, 0],
        [0, 0, 0, 0, 0]
])

start = grid.node(0, 0)
end = grid.node(4, 4)

finder = AStarFinder()
path, runs = finder.find_path(start, end, grid)
print(path)  # Output: [(0, 0), (0, 2), (1, 2), (2, 2), (3, 2), (4, 2), (4, 3), (4, 4)]
```

Combining Multiple Libraries

Combining multiple libraries can enhance your game engine's capabilities. Here are some tips for integrating multiple libraries:

Ensure Compatibility

Ensure that the libraries you choose are compatible with each other and the overall architecture of your game engine. Check for dependencies and potential conflicts.

Modular Design

Use a modular design to keep different libraries and their functionalities separate. This makes it easier to manage and update individual components.

Performance Optimization

Profile your engine regularly to identify performance bottlenecks. Optimize the integration of multiple libraries to ensure smooth performance.

Consistent Interfaces

Define consistent interfaces for interacting with different libraries. This makes it easier to integrate and switch between libraries without major code changes.

Testing and Debugging

Thoroughly test the integration of multiple libraries to identify and fix issues. Use debugging tools to troubleshoot and ensure smooth operation.

By integrating these third-party libraries, you can significantly enhance the capabilities of your game engine, providing powerful tools for graphics, physics, audio, AI, and more.

Chapter 17: Game Monetization Strategies

Understanding Game Monetization

Game monetization is the process of generating revenue from a game. This can be achieved through various methods, each with its own set of strategies and best practices. Understanding the different monetization options and how to implement them effectively is crucial for the financial success of your game.

One of the most common monetization strategies is in-game purchases. This includes selling virtual goods, such as skins, weapons, or other items that enhance the player's experience. These purchases can be purely cosmetic or provide in-game advantages. The key to successful in-game purchases is to offer items that players find valuable and are willing to pay for.

Another popular method is advertisements. Games can display ads at various points, such as between levels or during loading screens. Ads can be in the form of banners, interstitials, or rewarded videos. Rewarded videos are particularly effective as they offer players in-game rewards for watching ads, which can increase engagement and ad revenue.

Subscription models are also gaining traction in the gaming industry. This involves charging players a recurring fee to access premium content or features. Subscriptions can provide a steady stream of revenue and often include benefits like exclusive items, ad-free experiences, or early access to new content.

Implementing a freemium model is another common approach. In this model, the game is free to play, but players can purchase additional features or content. This lowers the barrier to entry, attracting a larger player base, and then monetizes a fraction of these players who are willing to pay for extras.

The premium model, where players pay upfront to download the game, is less common for mobile games but still relevant for PC and console games. This approach requires a compelling game that justifies the initial cost, often supported by strong marketing and positive reviews.

Crowdfunding is an alternative method, where developers raise funds from the community before the game's release. Platforms like Kickstarter or Indiegogo allow developers to present their game concept and receive financial backing from interested players. Successful crowdfunding campaigns can also generate early buzz and a dedicated player base.

Merchandising is another revenue stream, where game-related physical products like clothing, toys, or accessories are sold. This not only provides additional income but also enhances the game's brand and visibility.

To implement these strategies, it's important to analyze the target audience and tailor the monetization approach accordingly. Developers should ensure that monetization does not negatively impact the player experience. Balancing revenue generation with user satisfaction is key to maintaining a loyal player base and long-term success.

In-Game Purchases and Ads

In-game purchases, also known as microtransactions, are a widely used monetization strategy in modern gaming. They allow players to buy virtual goods using real money, enhancing their gaming experience. These purchases can range from cosmetic items, such as character skins and costumes, to functional items that provide gameplay advantages, like weapons, power-ups, or additional lives.

To implement in-game purchases, developers need to integrate a payment processing system within the game. This can be done using various platforms, such as Google Play's in-app billing or Apple's in-app purchase system. These platforms handle the financial transactions, providing a secure and convenient way for players to make purchases.

Designing in-game purchases requires a careful balance to avoid a "pay-to-win" scenario, where players who spend money gain significant advantages over those who do not. Cosmetic items that do not affect gameplay are a popular choice, as they allow players to personalize their experience without disrupting game balance. Offering a variety of items at different price points can also cater to a wider audience, from casual spenders to dedicated fans.

Advertisements are another common monetization method, allowing developers to generate revenue by displaying ads to players. There are several types of ads that can be integrated into a game:

1. **Banner Ads**: These are small ads that appear at the top or bottom of the screen. They are less intrusive but generate lower revenue compared to other ad formats.
2. **Interstitial Ads**: Full-screen ads that appear at natural breakpoints in the game, such as between levels. They are more engaging but can be disruptive if not implemented carefully.
3. **Rewarded Video Ads**: Players voluntarily watch video ads in exchange for in-game rewards, such as extra lives or in-game currency. This format is popular because it provides value to both players and developers.

To maximize ad revenue, developers can use ad mediation platforms that manage multiple ad networks, ensuring the highest-paying ads are displayed. It's also important to consider the frequency and placement of ads to avoid disrupting the player experience. Offering an ad-free version of the game for a one-time purchase can also be a viable option for players who prefer not to see ads.

Premium vs. Freemium Models

The premium and freemium models represent two distinct approaches to game monetization. Understanding their differences and potential benefits can help developers choose the right strategy for their game.

Premium Model

In the premium model, players pay an upfront fee to download and play the game. This approach is more common for PC and console games, where players are accustomed to purchasing games outright. The premium model can also work for mobile games, especially if the game offers high-quality content and a compelling experience.

Advantages:

1. **Revenue Assurance**: Developers receive revenue upfront, reducing financial risk.
2. **Perceived Value**: Players often perceive premium games as higher quality, which can enhance the game's reputation.
3. **Ad-Free Experience**: Players who pay upfront typically expect an ad-free experience, which can lead to higher satisfaction.

Challenges:

1. **Higher Barrier to Entry**: The upfront cost can deter potential players, limiting the game's audience.
2. **Marketing and Perception**: Convincing players to pay upfront requires strong marketing and positive reviews.

Freemium Model

The freemium model allows players to download and play the game for free, with optional in-game purchases for additional content or features. This model is prevalent in mobile gaming, attracting a large player base by lowering the barrier to entry.

Advantages:

1. **Wider Audience**: Free access attracts more players, increasing the potential for monetization through in-game purchases.
2. **Ongoing Revenue**: In-game purchases can provide a steady stream of revenue over time.
3. **Flexible Monetization**: Developers can offer various purchasing options, catering to different spending preferences.

Challenges:

1. **Monetization Balance**: Ensuring that in-game purchases do not disrupt game balance or create a pay-to-win scenario.
2. **Player Retention**: Keeping players engaged and encouraging spending without negatively impacting the experience.

Choosing the Right Model

The choice between premium and freemium depends on various factors, including the game's genre, target audience, and platform. For example, casual mobile games often succeed with the freemium model, while complex RPGs or story-driven games may benefit from a premium approach.

Hybrid models are also an option, combining elements of both strategies. For instance, a game might offer a free base version with optional premium expansions or additional content packs. This allows developers to attract a broad audience while providing opportunities for monetization.

Ultimately, the key to successful monetization is understanding the preferences and behaviors of the target audience. Conducting market research and analyzing player feedback can provide valuable insights into which model will work best for a particular game.

Marketing Your Game

Effective marketing is crucial for the success of any game, regardless of its monetization strategy. A well-executed marketing plan can generate awareness, attract players, and drive revenue. Here are some key components of a successful game marketing strategy:

1. Identify Your Target Audience

Understanding your target audience is the first step in creating a marketing plan. Identify the demographics, interests, and gaming habits of potential players. This information will guide your marketing efforts, ensuring that your messages resonate with the right people.

2. Create a Strong Brand

A strong brand helps your game stand out in a crowded market. Develop a compelling logo, tagline, and visual identity that reflect the game's theme and appeal to your target audience. Consistent branding across all marketing channels reinforces your game's identity and makes it more memorable.

3. Build a Website and Social Media Presence

A dedicated website serves as a central hub for information about your game. Include key details, such as features, screenshots, videos, and download links. Regularly update the website with news, updates, and blog posts to keep players engaged.

Social media platforms are essential for reaching and interacting with your audience. Create profiles on popular platforms like Facebook, Twitter, Instagram, and TikTok. Share updates, behind-the-scenes content, and engage with followers to build a community around your game.

4. Leverage Influencers and Streamers

Influencers and streamers can significantly impact your game's visibility and credibility. Identify influencers and streamers who align with your target audience and reach out for potential collaborations. They can create gameplay videos, reviews, and live streams, showcasing your game to their followers and generating buzz.

5. Participate in Gaming Communities

Engage with gaming communities on platforms like Reddit, Discord, and gaming forums. Participate in discussions, share updates, and seek feedback from players. Being an active member of these communities can help you build relationships with potential players and gain valuable insights.

6. Run Paid Advertising Campaigns

Paid advertising can boost your game's visibility and reach a larger audience. Consider running ads on platforms like Google Ads, Facebook Ads, and Twitter Ads. Use targeted advertising to reach specific demographics and track the performance of your campaigns to optimize results.

7. Create a Compelling Launch Campaign

A successful launch campaign can generate excitement and drive initial downloads. Plan a series of activities leading up to the launch, such as teaser trailers, beta tests, and countdowns. Consider offering pre-order bonuses or exclusive in-game items to incentivize early downloads.

8. Analyze and Optimize

Marketing is an ongoing process that requires continuous analysis and optimization. Use analytics tools to track the performance of your marketing efforts, including website traffic, social media engagement, and ad campaign results. Use this data to refine your strategy and improve future campaigns.

Legal and Ethical Considerations

When monetizing a game, it's important to consider the legal and ethical implications. Adhering to legal requirements and maintaining ethical standards helps build trust with players and ensures long-term success.

Legal Considerations

1. **Compliance with Laws and Regulations**: Ensure that your game complies with relevant laws and regulations, such as data protection laws, consumer protection laws, and advertising standards. This includes obtaining necessary licenses and adhering to age ratings.
2. **Intellectual Property Rights**: Respect intellectual property rights by avoiding the use of copyrighted material without permission. This applies to game assets, music, trademarks, and other content. Consider registering your own intellectual property to protect it from unauthorized use.

3. **Privacy and Data Protection**: Implement robust privacy policies and practices to protect player data. Inform players about the data you collect, how it is used, and obtain their consent where required. Ensure compliance with data protection laws, such as the GDPR or CCPA.
4. **Fair Advertising Practices**: Ensure that all advertisements are truthful and not misleading. Disclose any sponsored content or paid endorsements to maintain transparency with players.

Ethical Considerations

1. **Fair Monetization Practices**: Avoid implementing monetization strategies that exploit or deceive players. Ensure that in-game purchases offer fair value and do not create an imbalanced or unfair playing environment.
2. **Protecting Vulnerable Players**: Be mindful of vulnerable players, such as children or individuals with addictive tendencies. Implement measures to prevent excessive spending and encourage responsible gaming. Consider incorporating parental controls and spending limits.
3. **Transparent Communication**: Communicate transparently with players about monetization practices, game updates, and changes. Build trust by being honest and responsive to player concerns and feedback.
4. **Maintaining Game Integrity**: Ensure that monetization practices do not compromise the integrity of the game. Avoid pay-to-win mechanics that can frustrate non-paying players and damage the game's reputation.
5. **Community Engagement**: Foster a positive and inclusive community by promoting respectful behavior and addressing toxic behavior. Encourage player feedback and involve the community in decision-making processes.

By considering these legal and ethical aspects, developers can create a positive gaming experience that respects players' rights and fosters a loyal and engaged player base.

Chapter 18: Game Testing and Quality Assurance

Importance of Testing in Game Development

Testing is a critical phase in game development, ensuring that the final product is polished, functional, and free of major bugs. Proper testing helps developers identify and fix issues, improve gameplay, and deliver a high-quality experience to players.

1. Identifying Bugs and Glitches

Bugs and glitches can significantly impact a game's performance and player experience. Testing helps identify these issues early in the development process, allowing developers to address them before the game's release. Common types of bugs include graphical glitches, audio problems, gameplay errors, and performance issues.

2. Ensuring Gameplay Balance

Gameplay balance is crucial for creating a fair and enjoyable experience. Testing allows developers to evaluate the balance of game mechanics, such as character abilities, item effectiveness, and difficulty levels. By adjusting these elements, developers can ensure that the game is challenging but not frustrating, providing a rewarding experience for players.

3. Improving User Experience

User experience (UX) encompasses all aspects of a player's interaction with the game. Testing helps identify areas where the UX can be improved, such as intuitive controls, clear instructions, and smooth navigation. A positive UX enhances player satisfaction and retention.

4. Compatibility Testing

Games need to run smoothly across various devices and platforms. Compatibility testing ensures that the game functions correctly on different hardware configurations, operating systems, and screen sizes. This is particularly important for mobile games, which must accommodate a wide range of devices.

5. Performance Optimization

Performance issues, such as lag, crashes, and long loading times, can frustrate players and lead to negative reviews. Testing helps identify performance bottlenecks and optimize the game's performance. This includes optimizing code, reducing memory usage, and improving rendering efficiency.

6. Compliance and Certification

Many platforms and app stores require games to meet specific standards and pass certification tests before they can be published. Testing ensures that the game complies with these standards, avoiding delays or rejections during the submission process.

7. Feedback and Iteration

Testing provides valuable feedback from players and testers, which can guide further development. By iterating on this feedback, developers can refine the game, fix issues, and enhance features. This iterative process helps create a polished and engaging final product.

8. Building Player Trust

Releasing a well-tested game builds trust with players, leading to positive reviews, recommendations, and long-term success. A game that functions smoothly and delivers a satisfying experience encourages players to invest time and money, supporting the developer's efforts.

Automated Testing Techniques

Automated testing techniques can significantly streamline the testing process, allowing developers to identify and fix issues more efficiently. Automated tests are scripts or tools that simulate player interactions and check the game's behavior against expected outcomes. Here are some common automated testing techniques:

1. Unit Testing

Unit testing involves testing individual components or functions of the game in isolation. This helps ensure that each part of the game works correctly on its own. Unit tests are typically written by developers and can be run automatically as part of the development process.

```python
def test_player_health():
    player = Player()
    player.take_damage(10)
    assert player.health == 90
```

2. Integration Testing

Integration testing verifies that different components of the game work together as expected. This type of testing is essential for identifying issues that may arise when individual components interact. Integration tests can be automated to check the interactions between various systems, such as graphics, physics, and input handling.

```python
def test_player_pickup_item():
    player = Player()
    item = HealthPack()
    player.pick_up(item)
    assert player.health == 100
```

3. Regression Testing

Regression testing ensures that new code changes do not introduce new bugs or break existing functionality. Automated regression tests run a suite of tests on the game after each update, verifying that previously working features still function correctly. This helps maintain the stability of the game as it evolves.

4. Performance Testing

Performance testing evaluates the game's performance under various conditions, such as high player load or complex scenes. Automated performance tests can measure metrics like frame rate, memory usage, and load times, helping developers optimize the game's performance.

5. UI Testing

UI testing verifies that the game's user interface functions correctly and is intuitive for players. Automated UI tests simulate user interactions, such as clicking buttons and navigating menus, to ensure that the UI behaves as expected. This helps identify issues with controls, menus, and visual elements.

6. Load Testing

Load testing evaluates how the game performs under heavy load, such as many simultaneous players or complex scenarios. Automated load tests simulate large numbers of players or events, helping developers identify performance bottlenecks and scalability issues.

7. Continuous Integration

Continuous integration (CI) is a development practice where code changes are automatically tested and integrated into the main codebase. CI systems run automated tests on each code commit, ensuring that the game remains stable and functional throughout development. This helps catch issues early and maintain a high quality of code.

Automated testing techniques can save time and effort, allowing developers to focus on creating new features and improving the game. However, it's important to complement automated tests with manual testing to catch issues that automated tests may miss.

Bug Tracking and Management

Effective bug tracking and management are essential for maintaining the quality of a game throughout its development and post-release lifecycle. Here are some key practices for bug tracking and management:

1. Choosing a Bug Tracking Tool

A good bug tracking tool is crucial for managing and organizing reported issues. Popular bug tracking tools include JIRA, Trello, Bugzilla, and GitHub Issues. These tools allow developers to create, assign, prioritize, and track bugs, ensuring that all issues are addressed systematically.

2. Reporting Bugs

Encourage team members and testers to report bugs with detailed descriptions, including steps to reproduce, expected behavior, actual behavior, and any relevant screenshots or logs. Clear and comprehensive bug reports help developers understand and fix issues more efficiently.

3. Prioritizing Bugs

Not all bugs have the same level of severity or impact on the game. Prioritize bugs based on factors such as their impact on gameplay, frequency of occurrence, and player experience. Critical bugs that cause crashes or major disruptions should be addressed first, while minor cosmetic issues can be scheduled for later fixes.

4. Assigning Bugs

Assign bugs to the appropriate team members based on their expertise and availability. Ensure that everyone on the team is aware of their responsibilities and the current status of assigned bugs. Regularly review and update bug assignments to keep the process moving smoothly.

5. Tracking Bug Status

Track the status of each bug throughout its lifecycle, from reporting to resolution. Common status categories include New, In Progress, Resolved, and Closed. Keeping track of bug status helps the team stay organized and ensures that no issues are overlooked.

6. Testing Bug Fixes

After a bug is fixed, it's important to test the fix to ensure that the issue is resolved and that no new problems have been introduced. Automated regression tests can help with this, but manual testing is also necessary to verify the fix in real-world scenarios.

7. Communicating with the Team

Effective communication is key to successful bug management. Regularly update the team on the status of major bugs, upcoming releases, and any changes to the bug tracking process. Encourage collaboration and open communication to ensure that everyone is on the same page.

8. Analyzing Bug Trends

Analyzing bug trends can provide valuable insights into the development process and areas that need improvement. Identify common types of bugs, recurring issues, and patterns in bug reports. Use this information to refine development practices, improve testing procedures, and enhance the overall quality of the game.

9. Continuous Improvement

Bug tracking and management should be part of a continuous improvement process. Regularly review and update your bug tracking practices to ensure they remain effective and efficient. Encourage feedback from the team and be open to adopting new tools and techniques that can improve bug management.

By implementing these practices, developers can effectively manage bugs, maintain the quality of the game, and deliver a polished and enjoyable experience to players.

User Testing and Feedback

User testing and feedback are critical components of game development, providing valuable insights into how players interact with the game and identifying areas for improvement. Here are some key steps for conducting effective user testing and gathering feedback:

1. Defining Testing Objectives

Before conducting user testing, define clear objectives for what you want to achieve. This could include testing specific features, evaluating gameplay balance, or gathering feedback on the user interface. Having clear objectives helps focus the testing process and ensures that you gather relevant information.

2. Selecting Testers

Select a diverse group of testers that represent your target audience. This can include existing players, friends, family, or recruited testers from online communities. A varied group of testers provides a broad range of perspectives and helps identify different issues that may affect various player demographics.

3. Creating Test Scenarios

Create specific test scenarios that guide testers through different aspects of the game. These scenarios should cover a range of gameplay elements, such as tutorials, combat, puzzles, and user interface interactions. Providing structured scenarios helps ensure comprehensive testing and consistent feedback.

4. Conducting Playtests

During playtests, observe how testers interact with the game, noting any issues, frustrations, or areas of confusion. Encourage testers to think aloud and share their thoughts as they play. This real-time feedback provides valuable insights into the player's experience and helps identify areas for improvement.

5. Gathering Feedback

In addition to real-time observations, gather written feedback from testers through surveys or feedback forms. Ask specific questions about different aspects of the game, such as gameplay mechanics, story, graphics, and controls. Open-ended questions can also provide valuable qualitative feedback.

6. Analyzing Feedback

Analyze the feedback to identify common themes, issues, and areas for improvement. Look for patterns in the feedback that indicate recurring problems or opportunities for enhancement. Prioritize the most critical issues that impact gameplay and player satisfaction.

7. Iterating on Feedback

Use the feedback to make informed changes and improvements to the game. This iterative process involves addressing identified issues, refining gameplay mechanics, and enhancing the overall user experience. After making changes, conduct additional testing to verify that the improvements are effective.

8. Involving the Community

Engage with the game's community to gather ongoing feedback and involve players in the development process. Platforms like Discord, Reddit, and social media can facilitate communication with players and provide a channel for continuous feedback. Involving the community fosters a sense of ownership and loyalty among players.

9. Balancing Player Expectations

While player feedback is invaluable, it's important to balance player expectations with the overall vision for the game. Not all feedback may align with the intended design or direction. Use your judgment to determine which feedback to implement and how to integrate it without compromising the game's core experience.

10. Continuous Improvement

User testing and feedback should be an ongoing process throughout the development lifecycle. Regularly conducting playtests and gathering feedback helps ensure that the game evolves based on player input and remains engaging and enjoyable.

By implementing effective user testing and feedback practices, developers can create a game that resonates with players, delivers a satisfying experience, and achieves long-term success.

Ensuring Game Quality

Ensuring game quality is a comprehensive process that involves meticulous planning, testing, and refinement. Here are some essential practices to ensure the quality of your game:

1. Establish Quality Standards

Define clear quality standards for your game, including performance benchmarks, visual and audio quality, gameplay mechanics, and user experience. These standards serve as a baseline for evaluating the game's quality throughout development.

2. Create a Testing Plan

Develop a detailed testing plan that outlines the testing phases, objectives, and methodologies. Include various types of testing, such as unit testing, integration testing, performance testing, and user testing. A well-structured testing plan ensures thorough and systematic testing.

3. Automate Testing

Implement automated testing to streamline the testing process and identify issues early. Automated tests can cover repetitive and time-consuming tasks, such as regression testing and performance testing, allowing developers to focus on more complex testing scenarios.

4. Conduct Regular Playtests

Regular playtests with a diverse group of testers help identify issues that may not be apparent through automated testing. Playtests provide valuable feedback on gameplay, user experience, and overall enjoyment. Schedule playtests throughout the development cycle to gather continuous feedback.

5. Monitor Performance Metrics

Track performance metrics, such as frame rate, memory usage, and load times, to ensure the game meets performance standards. Use profiling tools to identify performance bottlenecks and optimize the game's performance.

6. Address Bugs Promptly

Implement a robust bug tracking and management system to document, prioritize, and address bugs promptly. Regularly review and update the status of reported bugs to ensure that critical issues are resolved before release.

7. Optimize User Experience

Focus on optimizing the user experience by ensuring intuitive controls, clear instructions, and smooth navigation. Pay attention to player feedback and make necessary adjustments to enhance the overall user experience.

8. Ensure Cross-Platform Compatibility

Test the game on various devices and platforms to ensure compatibility and consistent performance. This includes different screen sizes, operating systems, and hardware configurations. Address any platform-specific issues to provide a seamless experience for all players.

9. Verify Compliance

Ensure that the game complies with platform-specific guidelines, standards, and certification requirements. This includes age ratings, content guidelines, and technical standards set by app stores and gaming platforms.

10. Document Processes

Maintain thorough documentation of development processes, testing procedures, and quality standards. Documentation helps ensure consistency, facilitates onboarding of new team members, and provides a reference for future development.

11. Foster a Quality Culture

Promote a culture of quality within the development team by encouraging open communication, collaboration, and continuous improvement. Involve all team members in the quality assurance process and emphasize the importance of delivering a high-quality game.

By following these practices, developers can ensure that their game meets high-quality standards, providing players with an enjoyable, polished, and engaging experience.

Post-Release Support and Updates

Post-release support and updates are crucial for maintaining player engagement, addressing issues, and ensuring the long-term success of a game. Here are some key practices for effective post-release support and updates:

1. Monitor Player Feedback

Continuously monitor player feedback through reviews, forums, social media, and in-game feedback mechanisms. Pay attention to common issues, feature requests, and suggestions. Engaging with players and responding to their feedback builds trust and demonstrates a commitment to improving the game.

2. Release Regular Updates

Regular updates keep the game fresh and engaging for players. This can include bug fixes, performance improvements, new content, and gameplay enhancements. Establish a schedule for updates, such as monthly or quarterly, to ensure consistent improvements.

3. Address Critical Issues

Promptly address critical issues that impact gameplay, such as bugs, crashes, and performance problems. Prioritize these issues to minimize disruption for players and maintain a positive reputation.

4. Introduce New Content

Introducing new content, such as levels, characters, items, and events, keeps the game exciting and encourages continued play. Plan and develop new content based on player preferences and trends, ensuring that it aligns with the overall vision of the game.

5. Balance Gameplay

Regularly evaluate and adjust gameplay balance to ensure a fair and enjoyable experience for all players. This includes tweaking difficulty levels, adjusting item effectiveness, and balancing character abilities. Player feedback and data analytics can guide these adjustments.

6. Communicate with Players

Maintain open and transparent communication with players about upcoming updates, changes, and new content. Use in-game announcements, social media, and community forums to keep players informed and engaged. Acknowledge and address player concerns and feedback.

7. Implement Quality Assurance

Ensure that all updates and new content undergo thorough testing before release. This includes automated testing, manual testing, and user testing to identify and fix issues. A robust quality assurance process minimizes the risk of introducing new bugs and maintains the game's quality.

8. Analyze Player Data

Analyze player data to understand player behavior, preferences, and trends. Use this data to inform decisions about updates, content development, and gameplay adjustments. Data-driven insights help create a more engaging and satisfying player experience.

9. Offer Limited-Time Events

Limited-time events, such as special challenges, seasonal events, and exclusive rewards, create excitement and encourage player engagement. Plan and execute events that align with player interests and enhance the overall game experience.

10. Plan for Longevity

Consider the long-term vision for the game and plan updates and support accordingly. This includes setting goals for future content, expanding the game's universe, and exploring new monetization opportunities. A clear roadmap helps maintain player interest and support over time.

By implementing these practices, developers can ensure effective post-release support and updates, maintaining player engagement and achieving long-term success for their game.

Chapter 19: Publishing and Distribution

Preparing Your Game for Release

Preparing your game for release is a multifaceted process that involves polishing the game, ensuring it runs smoothly on target platforms, and creating the necessary assets and documentation for distribution. This preparation can be broken down into several key areas: final testing, optimization, packaging, and creating promotional materials.

Firstly, extensive testing is crucial. This involves not only bug testing but also ensuring the game provides a consistent and enjoyable experience across different devices and screen resolutions. Automated testing scripts can be useful for checking various game states, but human testers are invaluable for providing feedback on gameplay, balance, and overall feel.

Optimization is another critical step. This involves refining the game's code and assets to ensure it runs efficiently. Techniques such as reducing the size of textures, optimizing sound files, and minimizing the use of complex algorithms can help improve performance. Profiling tools can be used to identify bottlenecks and areas where performance can be enhanced.

Packaging your game is also essential. For PC games, this typically involves creating an installer or providing a zip file with the necessary executables and assets. For mobile games, this means preparing APK files for Android or IPA files for iOS, adhering to the specific guidelines and requirements of each platform.

Creating promotional materials is vital for generating interest in your game. This includes screenshots, trailers, and a compelling description of the game. These assets will be used on distribution platforms and social media to attract potential players. It's also helpful to have a press kit available for journalists and influencers who may want to cover your game.

Documentation should not be overlooked. This includes a readme file with installation instructions, a manual or help file explaining the game's mechanics, and a changelog detailing updates and fixes. Good documentation can enhance the player experience and reduce the number of support requests.

Finally, consider creating a demo version of your game. This allows players to try out a portion of the game for free, which can help build interest and drive sales. Ensure the demo is polished and representative of the final product to make a good impression on potential customers.

Choosing Distribution Platforms

Choosing the right distribution platforms is crucial for reaching your target audience and maximizing your game's visibility. There are several types of platforms to consider, each with its own advantages and challenges.

Digital storefronts like Steam, GOG, and the Epic Games Store are popular choices for PC games. These platforms offer a large user base and robust features for game distribution, including automatic updates, community features, and promotional tools. However, they also take a percentage of your sales, typically around 30%.

For mobile games, the primary platforms are the Apple App Store and Google Play Store. These stores provide access to millions of potential players, but the competition is fierce, and standing out can be challenging. Optimizing your game's store listing with high-quality visuals, a compelling description, and effective keywords is essential for visibility.

If you're developing for consoles, platforms like the PlayStation Store, Xbox Live, and the Nintendo eShop are your primary options. Console distribution often requires additional steps, such as obtaining developer kits, passing certification processes, and meeting platform-specific requirements. The potential rewards are significant, with access to dedicated gaming audiences and higher perceived value.

Independent distribution options include itch.io and Game Jolt, which are great for indie developers and smaller projects. These platforms typically take a smaller cut of your revenue and offer more flexibility in terms of pricing and distribution. They also foster strong community engagement, which can be beneficial for building a loyal player base.

Consider also the potential of emerging platforms like cloud gaming services (e.g., Google Stadia, Nvidia GeForce Now) and subscription services (e.g., Xbox Game Pass, PlayStation Now). These platforms can provide additional revenue streams and exposure, though they may require technical adjustments to your game.

Finally, your own website can serve as a distribution platform. This approach offers the most control over pricing and presentation but requires robust marketing efforts to drive traffic. Setting up a secure payment system and ensuring reliable hosting are essential for this method.

When choosing platforms, consider your target audience, the type of game you're distributing, and the resources you have available for marketing and support. Diversifying your distribution channels can help mitigate risks and maximize your game's reach.

Managing Digital Rights and DRM

Digital rights management (DRM) is a crucial aspect of game distribution, as it helps protect your intellectual property and prevent unauthorized copying and distribution. However, DRM can also affect the user experience, so it's important to choose and implement it carefully.

DRM solutions range from simple serial key checks to more complex systems that require online activation. Steamworks, for example, provides a comprehensive DRM solution integrated with the Steam platform, offering features like keyless activation and built-in piracy protection. However, it requires your game to be distributed through Steam.

For games distributed on multiple platforms, third-party DRM solutions like Denuvo or SecuROM can be used. These systems offer robust protection but can be controversial among players due to potential performance impacts and the requirement for an internet connection. It's important to balance the need for protection with maintaining a positive user experience.

Some developers opt for no DRM, relying on the goodwill of their players and the strength of their community to discourage piracy. This approach can be particularly effective for indie games and those with strong community engagement, where players are more likely to support the developers directly.

When implementing DRM, consider the potential impact on legitimate customers. Overly restrictive DRM can lead to frustration and negative reviews, which can harm your game's reputation and sales. Testing the DRM system thoroughly to ensure it does not interfere with gameplay or performance is essential.

In addition to DRM, consider implementing anti-cheat measures for multiplayer games. Solutions like Easy Anti-Cheat or BattlEye can help maintain a fair playing environment and protect your game from hackers and cheaters. These systems can also provide valuable analytics and insights into cheating patterns.

Regularly updating and patching your game is also important for maintaining security. Keeping your game up to date with the latest security fixes and improvements can help prevent vulnerabilities that could be exploited by pirates or cheaters.

Lastly, clear communication with your players about the reasons for using DRM and how it affects them can help mitigate negative perceptions. Transparency about your efforts to protect your intellectual property while maintaining a fair and enjoyable experience can foster goodwill and support from your community.

Marketing and Promotion

Marketing and promotion are critical components of a successful game launch. Without effective marketing, even the best game can go unnoticed. There are several strategies you can use to promote your game and reach a wider audience.

Firstly, building a strong online presence is essential. Create a dedicated website for your game, complete with information, screenshots, videos, and a blog to keep players updated on development progress. Social media platforms like Twitter, Facebook, and Instagram are also valuable tools for engaging with your audience and generating buzz.

Press outreach is another important aspect of marketing. Create a press kit that includes a press release, high-quality screenshots, a trailer, and a detailed description of your game. Reach out to gaming journalists, bloggers, and influencers who might be interested in covering your game. Personalized emails and follow-ups can help secure coverage and reviews.

Participating in game festivals and competitions can also provide valuable exposure. Events like PAX, GDC, and IndieCade offer opportunities to showcase your game to industry professionals and gamers alike. These events can also provide networking opportunities and valuable feedback from attendees.

Consider leveraging crowdfunding platforms like Kickstarter or Indiegogo to fund your game's development and build a community of supporters. Successful crowdfunding campaigns can provide both financial support and valuable marketing exposure. Be sure to create compelling campaign materials and set realistic goals and rewards.

Influencer marketing has become increasingly important in the gaming industry. Partnering with YouTubers, Twitch streamers, and other influencers who have a large following can help generate interest and drive sales. Provide influencers with early access to your game and encourage them to share their experiences with their audience.

Paid advertising can also be effective, particularly on platforms like Google Ads, Facebook Ads, and Reddit Ads. These platforms offer targeted advertising options that can help you reach your desired audience. Be sure to track the performance of your ads and adjust your strategy based on the results.

Community engagement is key to building a loyal player base. Create forums, Discord servers, or Reddit communities where players can discuss your game, share feedback, and interact with the development team. Active and responsive community management can foster a positive and supportive environment.

Finally, consider offering pre-orders or early access to generate early revenue and build anticipation for your game's release. Early access can also provide valuable feedback and help you identify and fix issues before the full launch.

Post-Release Support and Updates

Post-release support is crucial for maintaining player engagement and ensuring the long-term success of your game. This involves providing regular updates, addressing bugs and issues, and engaging with the community to gather feedback and make improvements.

Regular updates keep your game fresh and can help retain players. These updates can include new content, such as levels, characters, and features, as well as quality-of-life improvements based on player feedback. Establishing a roadmap for future updates and sharing it with your community can build anticipation and keep players invested.

Bug fixing is an ongoing process. Even with thorough testing, issues may arise after launch that need to be addressed promptly. Setting up a system for players to report bugs and providing timely responses can help maintain a positive relationship with your community. Regularly patching your game to fix these issues demonstrates your commitment to quality.

Engaging with your community is essential for gathering feedback and building loyalty. Actively participate in forums, social media, and other community platforms to listen to player concerns and suggestions. Transparency about your development process and upcoming updates can foster trust and goodwill.

boundaries, taking breaks, and prioritizing self-care can prevent burnout and keep you motivated.

10. Celebrate Milestones - Celebrating small victories and milestones along the development journey can boost morale and provide a sense of accomplishment. Recognizing progress, no matter how small, can keep you motivated and focused on your goals.

By learning from the experiences of indie developers, you can navigate the challenges of game development more effectively and increase your chances of creating a successful and enjoyable game.

Emerging Trends in Game Development

The game development industry is constantly evolving, with new trends and technologies shaping the way games are created and experienced. Staying informed about these emerging trends can help you stay competitive and innovative. Here are some of the key trends currently impacting game development:

1. Virtual Reality (VR) and Augmented Reality (AR) - VR and AR technologies continue to advance, offering new possibilities for immersive gameplay experiences. Developers are exploring innovative ways to integrate VR and AR into various genres, from first-person shooters to puzzle games. As hardware becomes more accessible, these technologies are likely to become more mainstream.

2. Cloud Gaming - Cloud gaming services like Google Stadia, Nvidia GeForce Now, and Xbox Cloud Gaming are gaining traction. These platforms allow players to stream games directly to their devices, reducing the need for high-end hardware. For developers, this means optimizing games for cloud performance and considering new distribution models.

3. Procedural Content Generation - Procedural content generation involves using algorithms to create game content dynamically. This trend is becoming more prevalent in genres like roguelikes and open-world games, where it can enhance replayability and provide unique experiences for each player. Tools and frameworks for procedural generation are becoming more sophisticated and accessible.

4. Cross-Platform Play - Cross-platform play allows players on different devices and consoles to play together. This trend is driven by player demand for a seamless gaming experience and has led to increased collaboration between platform holders. Developers need to consider cross-platform compatibility and testing to ensure a smooth experience for all players.

5. Artificial Intelligence (AI) and Machine Learning - AI and machine learning are being used to enhance various aspects of game development, from creating more realistic NPC behaviors to optimizing in-game economies. These technologies can also assist in playtesting and bug detection, improving the development process.

Lessons Learned from Indie Developers

Indie developers face unique challenges and opportunities in the game development industry. Learning from their experiences can provide valuable insights and help you navigate your own development journey. Here are some key lessons learned from successful indie developers:

1. Start Small and Iterate - Many indie developers recommend starting with small, manageable projects before tackling larger, more complex games. This approach allows you to learn and improve your skills incrementally. Iterating on your game based on feedback and testing can help you refine mechanics and improve the overall experience.

2. Focus on Core Mechanics - Successful indie games often have a strong focus on core mechanics that are polished and engaging. Prioritizing the development of these mechanics ensures that your game is fun and functional at its core. Additional features and content can be added later as the core gameplay solidifies.

3. Build a Community Early - Engaging with a community of players and supporters early in the development process can provide valuable feedback and build anticipation for your game. Platforms like Discord, Reddit, and social media can help you connect with potential players and gather input that shapes your game's development.

4. Manage Scope and Resources - Indie developers often work with limited resources, making it crucial to manage the scope of your project carefully. Setting realistic goals and milestones can help you stay on track and avoid burnout. Consider leveraging free or affordable tools and assets to reduce costs.

5. Embrace Failure and Learn - Failure is a natural part of the development process. Successful indie developers view failure as an opportunity to learn and improve. Analyzing what went wrong and how to fix it can lead to better decision-making and more resilient development practices.

6. Network and Collaborate - Building relationships with other developers, artists, and industry professionals can provide valuable support and opportunities. Collaborating with others can bring fresh perspectives and skills to your project. Participating in game jams and industry events can help you expand your network.

7. Marketing is Key - Effective marketing is crucial for the success of an indie game. Developers should invest time and effort into creating a strong online presence, reaching out to the press, and engaging with influencers. A well-executed marketing strategy can significantly boost your game's visibility and sales.

8. Adapt to Feedback - Being receptive to player feedback and willing to make changes based on that feedback is essential. Early access and beta testing phases can provide insights into what players enjoy and what needs improvement. Adaptability can lead to a better final product.

9. Maintain Work-Life Balance - The demands of game development can be intense, but maintaining a healthy work-life balance is important for long-term sustainability. Setting

Chapter 20: Case Studies and Future Trends

Successful PyGame Projects

Examining successful PyGame projects can provide valuable insights and inspiration for your own game development journey. PyGame has been used to create a wide range of games, from simple arcade-style games to complex simulations. Here are a few notable examples:

1. Solar Wolf - Developed by Pete Shinners, Solar Wolf is a retro-style arcade game where players collect boxes while avoiding enemies. The game's smooth gameplay, polished graphics, and engaging mechanics have made it a popular example of what can be achieved with PyGame. The source code is available for learning and modification, making it a great resource for aspiring developers.

2. Frets on Fire - A music rhythm game inspired by Guitar Hero, Frets on Fire allows players to play along with their favorite songs using a keyboard or a guitar controller. The game features customizable songs and a vibrant community of players who create and share new content. Frets on Fire showcases PyGame's ability to handle complex input and synchronization with music.

3. Dangerous High School Girls in Trouble - This narrative-driven game combines elements of board games, adventure games, and visual novels. Players navigate a 1920s high school, solving mysteries and building relationships with other characters. The game's unique art style and storytelling demonstrate PyGame's versatility in creating non-traditional game experiences.

4. Thousand Parsec - An open-source project, Thousand Parsec is a framework for building space-themed strategy games. It supports multiplayer gameplay, complex AI, and large-scale simulations. The project's modular design and extensive documentation make it a valuable resource for developers interested in creating strategy games with PyGame.

5. Retro Game Challenge - A collection of mini-games inspired by classic arcade titles, Retro Game Challenge offers a nostalgic experience with modern twists. Each mini-game features distinct mechanics and challenges, showcasing PyGame's flexibility in handling different game genres within a single project.

These examples highlight the diverse possibilities of PyGame. By studying the source code, design choices, and development processes of successful projects, you can gain valuable insights into best practices and innovative techniques. Additionally, contributing to open-source PyGame projects can provide hands-on experience and help you build a portfolio of work.

Consider implementing live events or seasonal content to keep your game engaging. Limited-time events, special challenges, and holiday-themed updates can attract players back to your game and provide new experiences. These events can also create opportunities for additional revenue through in-game purchases or special offers.

Monitoring player data and analytics can provide valuable insights into how players are interacting with your game. This data can help you identify areas where players are struggling or losing interest, allowing you to make targeted improvements. Tools like Google Analytics, Unity Analytics, or custom-built solutions can be used to track player behavior.

Post-release marketing is also important. Continue promoting your game through social media, press releases, and community engagement. Positive reviews and word-of-mouth recommendations can drive new sales long after the initial launch. Consider offering discounts or bundles to attract new players and boost sales.

Providing support and addressing player concerns promptly can help maintain a positive reputation. Setting up a support system, such as a dedicated email address or a ticketing system, allows players to reach out with issues or questions. Providing clear and helpful responses can enhance the player experience and reduce frustration.

Finally, consider the long-term future of your game. If it proves successful, you may want to develop sequels, spin-offs, or downloadable content (DLC). Planning for these possibilities early can help you build a sustainable development strategy and continue to grow your player base.

6. Blockchain and NFTs - Blockchain technology and non-fungible tokens (NFTs) are starting to make an impact in the gaming industry. Blockchain can enable secure in-game transactions and ownership, while NFTs allow for unique digital assets that players can own and trade. However, this trend is still controversial and developers should consider the implications carefully.

7. Accessibility and Inclusivity - There is a growing emphasis on making games more accessible and inclusive. This includes designing games that can be played by people with disabilities, offering customizable controls, and providing diverse representation in characters and stories. Developers are increasingly prioritizing accessibility features and seeking feedback from diverse player groups.

8. Hyper-Casual Games - Hyper-casual games, characterized by their simple mechanics and short play sessions, have gained popularity on mobile platforms. These games are easy to pick up and play, making them appealing to a broad audience. The development cycle for hyper-casual games is often shorter, allowing for rapid experimentation and iteration.

9. Esports and Competitive Gaming - Esports continues to grow as a major industry, with professional leagues, tournaments, and a dedicated fanbase. Developers are creating games specifically designed for competitive play, with features that support streaming, spectating, and tournament organization. This trend is also driving the development of tools for balancing and matchmaking.

10. Sustainable Game Development - Environmental sustainability is becoming a consideration in game development. This includes optimizing code for energy efficiency, using eco-friendly hosting solutions, and raising awareness about environmental issues through game content. Developers are exploring ways to reduce the environmental impact of game development and distribution.

By staying informed about these emerging trends, developers can adapt to changes in the industry, explore new opportunities, and create innovative and engaging games that resonate with players.

The Future of PyGame

The future of PyGame looks promising as the community continues to grow and evolve. PyGame remains a popular choice for beginners and hobbyists due to its simplicity and ease of use. Here are some key areas where PyGame is likely to see developments in the future:

1. Enhanced Documentation and Tutorials - As the PyGame community expands, there will be a greater emphasis on creating comprehensive documentation and tutorials. This will help new developers get started more easily and provide advanced users with deeper insights into the library's capabilities.

2. Integration with Modern Python Features - PyGame will continue to integrate with modern Python features and libraries. This includes compatibility with the latest versions of Python and support for new Python features, such as async and await, which can improve the performance and responsiveness of games.

3. **Improved Performance** - Performance optimizations will be a focus for future PyGame releases. This includes reducing the overhead of rendering and input handling, as well as optimizing the underlying C code. Improved performance will enable developers to create more complex and visually appealing games.

4. **Expanded Community Resources** - The PyGame community is likely to produce more open-source projects, tools, and libraries that extend the functionality of PyGame. These resources will provide developers with additional capabilities and make it easier to implement common game features.

5. **Cross-Platform Development** - PyGame will continue to improve its support for cross-platform development. This includes better compatibility with mobile platforms, such as Android and iOS, and enhanced support for deployment on various desktop operating systems. Cross-platform development will enable developers to reach a wider audience with their games.

6. **Integration with Other Libraries** - PyGame will see increased integration with other popular Python libraries, such as Pyglet and Kivy. This will allow developers to leverage the strengths of multiple libraries in their projects and create more versatile and feature-rich games.

7. **Educational Use** - PyGame will remain a valuable tool for education, with more schools and coding bootcamps incorporating it into their curricula. The simplicity and hands-on nature of PyGame make it an excellent choice for teaching programming and game development concepts.

8. **Community Events and Competitions** - The PyGame community will continue to host events and competitions, such as game jams and hackathons. These events provide opportunities for developers to showcase their skills, collaborate with others, and receive feedback on their projects.

9. **Focus on Accessibility** - There will be a greater focus on making PyGame more accessible to a diverse range of developers. This includes creating tools and resources for developers with disabilities and ensuring that the PyGame library itself is easy to use and understand.

10. **Innovative Game Projects** - As more developers adopt PyGame, we can expect to see a wide variety of innovative game projects that push the boundaries of what can be achieved with the library. These projects will inspire others and demonstrate the versatility and power of PyGame.

The future of PyGame is bright, with continued growth and innovation driven by a passionate and dedicated community. Whether you are a beginner looking to create your first game or an experienced developer seeking new challenges, PyGame offers a versatile and accessible platform for game development.

Continuing Your Game Development Journey

Continuing your game development journey involves constant learning, experimentation, and growth. Here are some strategies to help you advance your skills and achieve your goals:

1. Keep Learning - The world of game development is always evolving, with new tools, techniques, and trends emerging regularly. Stay updated by reading articles, watching tutorials, and participating in online courses. Platforms like Coursera, Udemy, and YouTube offer a wealth of resources to expand your knowledge.

2. Build a Portfolio - Creating a portfolio of your work is essential for showcasing your skills and attracting potential employers or collaborators. Include a variety of projects that demonstrate your versatility and expertise. Make sure to highlight your best work and provide detailed descriptions of each project.

3. Collaborate with Others - Working with other developers, artists, and designers can enhance your skills and lead to new opportunities. Join game development communities, attend meetups, and participate in game jams to connect with like-minded individuals. Collaboration can also lead to the creation of more polished and ambitious projects.

4. Experiment with Different Genres and Styles - Exploring different game genres and art styles can help you discover new techniques and expand your creative horizons. Don't be afraid to step out of your comfort zone and try something new. This experimentation can lead to innovative ideas and unique game concepts.

5. Seek Feedback and Iterate - Feedback is invaluable for improving your work. Share your projects with others and seek constructive criticism. Use this feedback to iterate and refine your games. Continuous improvement is key to developing high-quality games that resonate with players.

6. Stay Motivated - Game development can be challenging, and it's important to stay motivated throughout the process. Set achievable goals, celebrate small victories, and take breaks when needed. Surround yourself with supportive individuals who encourage and inspire you.

7. Explore Advanced Topics - As you gain experience, delve into advanced topics such as artificial intelligence, procedural generation, and multiplayer networking. These areas offer opportunities to create more complex and engaging games. Advanced knowledge can also make you more competitive in the job market.

8. Share Your Knowledge - Teaching others is a great way to solidify your understanding and contribute to the community. Write tutorials, create video lessons, or mentor aspiring developers. Sharing your knowledge can also help you build a reputation as an expert in your field.

9. Stay Open to Opportunities - Be open to new opportunities that come your way, whether it's a job offer, a collaboration request, or a chance to speak at an event. Embracing these opportunities can lead to new experiences and help you grow as a developer.

10. Enjoy the Journey - Game development is a rewarding and creative endeavor. Enjoy the process, take pride in your accomplishments, and remember why you started creating games in the first place. Passion and enthusiasm are the driving forces behind successful game development.

Continuing your game development journey is a lifelong pursuit filled with challenges and rewards. By staying committed to learning, collaborating, and experimenting, you can achieve your goals and create games that inspire and entertain players around the world.